Nurturing for Community

306.8 Dunn, Dick
D
    Willing to try again

DATE DUE			
MAR. 26 1986			

WILLING TO TRY AGAIN

Steps Toward Blending a Family

Dick Dunn

WILLING TO TRY AGAIN

Steps Toward Blending a Family

Dick Dunn

Judson Press ® *Valley Forge*

WILLING TO TRY AGAIN: STEPS TOWARD BLENDING A FAMILY

Copyright © 1993
Judson Press, Valley Forge, PA 19482-0851
Second Printing, 1994

Library of Congress Cataloging-in-Publication Data

Dunn, Dick, 1934–
  Willing to try again : steps toward blending a family / by Dick Dunn.
  p.   cm.
  ISBN 0-8170-1185-4
  1. Stepfamilies – United States.   2. Remarriage – United States.
I. Title.
HQ759.92.D86   1993
306.874–dc20   92-33555
                                                                    CIP

To my wife, Betty, who patiently struggled
to learn these lessons with me.
And to our children,
Robert Arndt, and Kim and Scott Dunn.

Acknowledgments

In the writing of this book I am completely indebted to the stepfamily groups at Roswell United Methodist Church in Roswell, Georgia, where I serve as Minister of Singles and Stepfamilies. I knew some things about stepfamilies from personal experience, but they have taught me much more. Without them, this book could never have been written.

During the process of writing this book, I have felt God's guiding Spirit frequently, however, never more clearly than one Sunday after church when I attended a luncheon for new members. I happened to sit at a table with an attorney who introduced herself as Sandra Gray. That very week I had been struggling with a chapter in the book on prenuptial agreements and wills. I realized how little I really knew about the legal aspects of such things. Therefore, after talking a bit, I asked Sandra if she would be willing to read what I had written and give me some ideas about how to improve it.

Not only did Sandra give me additional ideas about prenuptial agreements and wills, she did a marvelous job of correcting and editing my writing. When we had finished the work on that chapter, I asked her if she would be willing to help me with the entire book. She said that she would love to do it. I do not think I have ever seen so much red ink. As she handed me the edited copy, Sandra told me in her kind way, "These are just suggestions. Use only what you find helpful."

I found about 90 percent of her wonderful corrections most helpful and never realized before how important a good editor is to a manuscript. I am deeply indebted to Sandra Gray for all of her valuable assistance.

I also want to give thanks to the senior minister at Roswell United Methodist Church, Dr. Malone Dodson. He was most supportive throughout the writing of this book, and without his encouragement there would never have been a stepfamily ministry at the church.

Contents

Introduction

Hardly a day goes by that I do not get a phone call from someone wanting to know about the stepfamily program at our church. Most of these calls are from people who are somewhat desperate. I can hear it in their voices. Their marriage has not turned out to be what they planned, expected, or anticipated. They are not sure that they can even stay married. Most of those who call have been married for only a few months, but a few have been married for a year or more. They are crying out for help.

Consider the following situation.

John and Sarah came to our stepfamily support group after they had been married approximately five months. This was Sarah's first marriage, but John had been married previously, divorced ten years later, and now had custody of the two children from that marriage, ages seven and five. John's first wife, Ann, had the children every other weekend and for two weeks in the summer. When John and Sarah first talked of marriage, they could not even imagine that the children would be any problem for them. Sarah loved children, and John seemed like a very devoted father, doing a remarkable job as a single parent while holding down a responsible employment position.

Certainly, things were sometimes a little less than orderly at
their house, but John hardly had time with all that he was doing. Sarah believed that she would be able to organize things
better once they were married.

Sarah called me some five months after they were married.
She had read in the newspaper that our church offered support
groups for stepfamilies. I gave her information about our
groups and invited her to the next meeting. Both Sarah and
John came to that meeting, and the tension that had developed
within their relationship was evident.

Sarah felt that the children did not like her, did not show
her respect, would not listen to her, and that John almost always took the children's side in any dispute. She was frustrated
most of the time, looked forward to those brief times that the
children were away, and was not sure that she really knew or
liked this man she had married.

John was also frustrated. This was not at all what he expected when he married. He felt trapped in the middle between
people he loved. However, while he loved all of them, they did
not seem to be able to love each other. He was sure that if Sarah
would just be a little more understanding and tolerant, everything would be fine. After all, children are only children. To
him, their behavior seemed perfectly normal. He felt Sarah expected too much from the kids.

Hearing them talk brought smiles to many within the
group, because most of us had experienced these same things —
maybe not in exactly the same way as John and Sarah, but
close enough. One man in the group had been quoted in a newspaper article on stepfamilies as saying, "The first year is terrible." Within our group, that had become a standard phrase.
When John and Sarah told their story, he quickly chimed in,
"The first year is terrible." The group broke up in laughter.
After we shared with John and Sarah the background of that
statement, many told of similar experiences and began to show
this couple some of the things that could help.

Before John and Sarah left that evening, the tension had
broken. Much of their anxiety had disappeared. They began to
see that their situation was typical of stepfamilies in general.
Within just a few months, John and Sarah were helping other
new couples by sharing those things that had been helpful to

them. This same couple, who three months earlier were talking about divorce, were now working together on the mutual task of making their stepfamily into something everyone could enjoy.

A stepfamily is simply a family where one or both of the marriage partners has children from a previous marriage. The United States Census Bureau predicts that by the turn of the century, stepfamilies will be the most common form of family life in the United States. One-third of all children born in the 1980s will be part of a stepfamily before they graduate from high school. Whether or not these children actually live in the home on a permanent basis has little to do with their impact upon the family. In some ways, noncustodial children and adult children can actually have a greater effect upon stepfamilies than children who live with the couple.

Many who have never experienced stepfamily living have a difficult time understanding that a subsequent marriage is very different from a first marriage. We often speak of "blended families" rather than "stepfamilies" because it sounds more positive and helps us picture a nice family unit again. However, families do not blend easily, and many stepfamilies never blend completely. Nevertheless, even when stepfamilies do not blend, they can become something of value to all concerned.

Throughout this book, I use the words "subsequent marriage." For some, these words may seem strange. I use them rather than "second marriage" simply because there are many who have married for the third or fourth time. This seems to be something we do not talk about or admit readily (especially within churches), but it is true. Therefore, I use subsequent marriage to mean any marriage after the first one.

A subsequent marriage has a better chance for success when certain things happen prior to the wedding, and I commend those who are reading this book in preparation for marriage. Hoping for a successful marriage without proper preparation is like trying to bake a cake without all of the ingredients. You are certain to end up with something, but it is not likely to resemble what you intended or hoped to have.

For those who have already married and are now experiencing some difficulties, welcome to reality. Like you, my wife, Betty, and I began our stepfamily with no idea that stepfamilies were any different from first-marriage families. Today, I am constantly amazed at just how different this marriage is from my first one. In many ways, it is so much better—more than I could have imagined. After all, I am older and better able to appreciate the things we do together and what we offer one another. While Betty and I have much in common, I am also able to enjoy her as an individual, different from myself, and I am not threatened by those differences. In this marriage, I am relaxed, confident, hopeful, and extremely happy.

It has taken our marriage several years to reach this point. The early years were often tumultuous. In spite of the fact that we loved each other and shared a common faith, we seemed powerless to overcome the multitude of complications that we experienced. There were unresolved problems from our first marriages. During our single lives, strong bonds had formed with our children that could not be easily shared. There were family relationships and influences that had not been foreseen. I was in the midst of a career change, and my financial condition was a shambles. Some of the children were less than thrilled about the marriage and found ways to let that be known, forcing us to take sides. The bond of love that we felt for one another and the faith that we shared was stretched to the limit. Consequently, there were periods during those early years when I was sure that we would soon be numbered among the people who had failed at marriage more than once. If we had not received help, I am certain we would have divorced.

The tragic truth is that most subsequent marriages fail. The obstacles involved are enormous. Without experience to draw upon, most of us are in over our heads without any understanding of what to do or how to do it. I thank God that during this time Betty and I were able to talk about it with people who understood. We found help both through counseling and through a support group of other people in subsequent marriages.

One of the things we discovered was that our situation was certainly not unique; in fact, it is shared by most people in such marriages. Those early years can be, and usually are, very difficult, but they are not impossible. With even a little help, most of the obstacles quickly become stepping stones upon which to build a wonderful future. Hearing about the various stepfamily struggles, someone once asked, "What chance do people have for success in these marriages?" The best answer to that is another question—"With or without help?" It makes all the difference whether a couple attempts to try it on their own or whether they admit from the start that subsequent marriages are difficult and that they will probably need assistance. This book is written to provide some of that help.

Subsequent marriages can be everything you hoped for and more. This will not just happen, however. It will take much work, much prayer, much patience, and more love and understanding than you thought you had to give. Actually, that is what will make it good. As you work together to make it so, you will come to a deeper appreciation of the person you have married. You will discover truths about love you probably never realized before, and your marriage will grow accordingly.

Chapter 1

Children and Stepfamilies

It is impossible to know how an individual child will react to one or both of his or her parents marrying again. There are simply too many variables, and there have not yet been many good studies done to assist us in our understanding. Therefore, it is important to appreciate that children can view an approaching marriage involving one of the parents with a variety of emotions, manifested through many different behaviors. As a rule, I often tell couples that when there are three children involved, they can expect one to be all for it, one to be set against it, and the third to be ambivalent, switching back and forth. These roles are not fixed and often change from child to child during the first three years of the marriage.

The age of the children is an important factor. Smaller children seem to adjust and accept stepfamily living more readily than older ones. However, we need to be cautious about such a conclusion, because it can also be that smaller children simply do not have the skills to express dissatisfaction as obviously as older ones do. Most couples find that adolescents and teenagers give them the most difficulty, but then again, that is true in first-marriage families also.

Frequently couples are fooled into believing that they will

have no problems with the children, either because the children are all in favor of the marriage or because they will have no children living with them. Both of these assumptions can come crashing down around the couple in the first few months of marriage. In the first case, where the children seem all in favor of the marriage, it is important to understand that what the children favor is a fantasy they have about what this new family will be like. Usually they anticipate a family like the one they had before, or if they do not remember that one, a family similar to those represented by some of their friends. Seldom do they anticipate any of the struggles and problems most stepfamilies encounter. Therefore, when their fantasy bubble breaks because reality does not live up to their expectations, their favor quickly turns to frustration, followed by anger. Over and over, I have seen couples who were absolutely amazed at how much and how quickly their children changed in regard to the new family.

In the second scenario, where no children live in the home, it is important to understand that the strong parent/child bond that exists between a biological parent and his or her children is not shared by the stepparent. While those children do not live in the home on a permanent basis, they will certainly visit there periodically and perhaps regularly.

All children within stepfamilies have experienced a major loss in their lives, either through the death of a parent or through the divorce of their parents. Frequently they receive very little assistance with the emotional struggle involved. Parents are usually struggling so much with their own emotions at these times that they have little energy left to help the children with their struggle. Most parents try, but they typically feel very inadequate for the task. It is not surprising that more and more children, even adult children, are seeing therapists and counselors to assist with this experience.

A Child's Special Relationship with a Single Parent

Because parents are very aware of their children's pain, and also because of their own struggle, something happens during the time following a divorce or the death of a mate that directly affects the experience of remarriage. Most single parents do not have the energy nor the inclination to constantly correct the children. Sensing great vulnerability in the children, most loving parents try to build them up, not tear them down. Also, parents want a time of peace while they are at home, and discipline would jeopardize that peace. Therefore, many single parents simply become close "friends" with their children, abandoning the old parenting role that is just not practical alone. While children thrive on the closeness developed with the single parent, this experience also preconditions some of the negative emotions that develop in stepfamilies.

Look at Amy. She was only seven when her parents divorced. She could not understand what she had done wrong, but she knew that she must have done something pretty bad to make her father leave. Her mother cried a lot, and Amy would usually cry along, her mother holding her close and saying something like, "Oh, I'm so glad that I still have you." Sometimes, they would even talk about her dad. Her mother assured her that the divorce had nothing to do with her, but Amy still believed that he would never have gone if she had been a better girl. Amy feared that her mother might leave also.

As time went on, some of Amy's fears began to subside. She saw her father regularly, and he seemed to enjoy these times with her very much. They played together and actually went more places than they ever had before. At home, her mother cried less and less. Amy's favorite time of the day was when she and her mother would sit together in the evening, talking, reading, or watching TV, with her mother's arm around her. Then, when Amy went to bed, her mother would allow her to sleep in the "big bed." Her mother had started letting Amy sleep with her shortly after Amy's father left. Amy liked that, feeling more secure with her mother there. Her mother seemed to like it, also, frequently putting her arm around her in the night. In some ways, Amy felt closer to both her mother and father than before. She hoped that it would not be long until her dad came back and they could all be together again.

One weekend Amy was surprised to find another woman at Dad's apartment. "This is Denise," he told her. "She is going to the zoo with us today."

Amy did not know what to say, so she said nothing.

Why? was all she could wonder. We don't need her, and I don't want her, was what she thought. What would Mom say if she knew?

Throughout the weekend, Amy was unusually quiet. "What's wrong?" her dad asked several times.

"Oh, I have a headache," Amy said. This was what she usually said when she did not want to talk, and most of the time it worked.

When Amy's mother picked her up on Sunday afternoon, it was obvious that something was not right. "What's the matter?" her mother asked as they were driving home. Amy began to sob. "What is it?" her mother prodded.

"I don't know how to tell you this," Amy replied.

"Just tell me," her mother said.

Through her sobbing, Amy burst out, "Dad had another woman with him at his apartment." She had been worrying for two days about how to break the news to her mother, knowing that it would be awful.

To her surprise, her mother took the news pretty well. "That's all right, honey," she said. "Your father and I are divorced now. He's allowed to see other women, and I'm allowed to see other men."

"You wouldn't, would you?" asked Amy.

"Oh, I might someday," her mother replied. "I miss having someone around the house."

"But I'm somebody," said Amy.

"Of course you are, honey," her mother said. "I mean, I miss having a man with us like we had before your father left."

"Why can't Dad just come back to live with us again?" asked Amy.

"That's not going to happen, honey." Amy's mother told her. "Remember how I said that your father and I are divorced now? Well, when people divorce, they often go on to marry other people."

"I sure hope Dad doesn't marry that woman," Amy said.

"Why? Wasn't she nice?" asked her mother.

"Oh, I guess she was all right," said Amy. "It's just that I like having Dad to myself when I go over there. We weren't alone the entire weekend."

Well, Amy's father did marry Denise, and two years later Amy's mother married again also. When that happened, Amy experienced grief all over again—the loss of the new relationship she had developed with her parents. While the divorce was extremely traumatic for Amy, their remarriages were equally difficult. She adapted to the divorce by becoming close friends with each of her parents. Now, each of them had someone else and did not need her for emotional support anymore. When her dad married, at least she still had her mother as a "best friend." However, when her mother married, that relationship began to change also. Each of her parents seemed to want to return to the way things were before the divorce, but with other people. Amy did not like that. If she could not have her mother and father together as parents, she did not want other people pretending to be her parents. Why did these strangers think they could tell her what to do? She wasn't their child.

A factor that many people in stepfamilies fail to understand is that most children, while longing for the home life they once shared with both parents, hate to give up the new friendship they have developed with their parents following a divorce or death. When parents marry someone else, it seems to children that they have lost both their former family and their closest friends. In a way, they have. While there is probably no practical way to avoid this loss for children, they can be assisted with their feelings of grief.

Change in Family Position

Tom anticipated the upcoming marriage of his mother very differently than Amy did. Tom's father had died when he was seven. Although Tom was close to his mother, he was very sad that he did not have a father like most of the other boys did. Four years after Tom's father died, his mother began dating a man named John, and Tom enjoyed the many things they all did together. He even invited John to go with his scout troop on a camping trip. For Tom, his mother's marriage would give him the father he missed.

Tom's older brother, Pete, was not as enthusiastic about his mother's remarriage. Pete had been eleven when his father died and was now fifteen. He had been the "man of the house" since his dad's death and felt that things were just fine the way they were. John was nice enough, but why was he necessary? Pete could see that Tom was excited about the marriage, but Pete felt displaced. Although Pete had hurt terribly when his father died, he had survived, partly because he was important to his mother and brother. Now, they did not seem to need him anymore. Well, he would be going off to college in a couple of years, anyway. If this is what they wanted, they could have it. He was not going to get involved.

John and the boys' mother, Kate, were aware of how the boys felt and did their best to help them with the transition. John took a real interest in Pete's school activities, going out of his way to be a friend. What shocked them most after the wedding was how Tom's attitude changed. Prior to the marriage, Tom was all for it, counting the days until John moved in. A couple of months after they were married, Tom seemed to do an about-face. It was almost a year before they could understand what had happened. John also had a son from a previous marriage who was eight years old. Since he lived in the same town, Henry was at their house almost every week, sometimes for several days at a time. While Tom had met Henry prior to the marriage, he had not spent much time with him. Now, they were together often, and Henry was the youngest. Suddenly, Tom had also lost his position in the family. He did not know where he fit, nor how to act. In this new family, Tom was a middle child.

Children can react to the remarriage of their parents in many ways. Much of their response will depend upon how they adapted to the loss following the divorce or death. Even then, it is important to understand that their attitude prior to the marriage may change after the marriage, depending on how the reality differs from their expectations. It may be impossible to discover this difference until the marriage is a fact. Children who seem excited and overjoyed before the wedding are sometimes displeased later. Those who are obviously upset beforehand may adapt quickly.

Reaction of Adult Children

Older children will also have mixed reactions to the remarriage of one of their parents. The fact that the children are themselves adults does not mean that they will quickly and easily adjust to or accept the new spouse. Often, their reaction will depend on how well they have dealt with their own grief following the divorce or death. While some grown children are thrilled with Mom or Dad's decision to marry again, others are horrified. It is difficult to predict.

When Frances heard that her mother was dating someone seriously, she prayed every day that they would marry. She had seen how lonely her mother had been since the divorce, and Frances longed for her to be happy again. Finally, it seemed that she was indeed happy, and Frances was delighted. Thelma, on the other hand, was not at all pleased. Thelma was the thirty-year-old daughter of the man Frances's mother was marrying. Thelma believed that her father was being misled again. He had been divorced twice already. Couldn't he see that the only thing women wanted from him was his money? She had only met Frances's mother once, but she had already decided that she did not like her.

These two daughters viewed the same marriage from two different perspectives. The big difference was that Frances had moved past the grief of her parents' divorce while Thelma had not. Frances had seen her father marry again and knew that he was happy in his new life. She also had seen how unhappy her mother had been for several years. Now, things were changing for her. Frances was relieved, believing that her mother could get on with her own life and Frances could stop worrying about her.

Thelma, in contrast, was still bitter over her parents' divorce. Both of them had married again within a year, and nothing was ever the same for Thelma. Holidays were especially difficult. Trying to take the children to see both of her parents, plus her husband's parents, was just too much. While Thelma had tried to like her father's second wife, when they were divorced some eight months later, all Thelma could see was how much that marriage had cost her father, financially and emotionally. She believed that this new marriage would be no better. By the time her father quit trying to make marriage work, there would probably be no inheritance left for her either.

Children of any age are affected greatly by the divorce or death of their parents. It is perfectly normal to react strongly to such an event. Children are also affected when their parents marry again, which causes another major disruption in their lives. It should not be surprising that they often respond negatively. When we realize how dramatically a subsequent marriage affects their lives, a situation over which they have almost no control, it should be more surprising when children react to a parent's remarriage in a positive way. Therefore, children need help with accepting the new marriage and understanding the positive benefits it can have for them.

Additionally, children of any age have a difficult time seeing their parents as sexual beings. Teenagers, wrestling with their own sexuality, are likely to be confused and surprised to discover that sex is also of interest to older people. Adult children frequently cannot fathom their parents doing "it." They are probably going to have difficulty for some time even with displays of affection in their presence. It seems easier to believe that parents simply have platonic relationships.

Foreseeable Problems and Suggested Solutions

Problem #1—Changing Rules

One confusing thing for many children is that the rules they have lived under for some time usually change following a remarriage. As mentioned earlier, single parenting is often quite different from parenting in nuclear families. In single-parent homes, children are much more involved in decisions that parents alone decide in nuclear families. Decisions about eating, cleaning, sleeping, and all the other daily routines of a home are seldom set down as laws that must be obeyed but are negotiated and talked about, with the children having considerable input. Therefore, rules in single-parent homes often become mutual decisions that do not even seem like rules.

However, when parents marry again, there is usually an attempt to return to the earlier family structure where the adults decide what should be done and how it should be done, simply telling the children their decisions. Stepparents are sometimes horrified at how loose everything seems to be in the single-parent home, with everyone (children included) doing whatever he or she wants, whenever he or she wants to do it.

To an outsider, a single-parent home may seem to have no structure at all. This certainly is not true. The structure in a single-parent home is simply different. However, even the single parent is usually ready to return to a more traditionally structured situation; therefore, once they are married, the adults often try to revert to the nuclear family structure. When this happens, children can become very upset at how much they are expected to change just to please this new person who has come to live with them.

Suggested Solution—Go Slowly

Biological parents and stepparents need to understand and appreciate how much is being asked of children in a stepfamily situation. Certainly, changes will need to be made in the rule structure. What worked during single parenting will probably not even be possible in a stepfamily. However, parents and stepparents need to go slowly, understanding that these changes will probably be very difficult for the children. Parents need to choose their battles carefully, considering just which rules are most important and which can be delayed for a while. Trying to change everything at once will undoubtedly lead to major conflict. Working with just one or two changes at a time will be easier for everyone and will meet with less resistance.

Problem #2—No Time Alone with the Biological Parent

Many children have expressed the concern that after their mother or father married again, they spent no time alone with the biological parent. During the time of single parenting, there is usually a great amount of time spent alone with the children. After a remarriage, this personal interaction often drops immediately to almost none. Having lost something that had come to mean so much to them, children see the stepparent as coming between them and their parent. In a real sense they are right, and they resent it.

Suggested Solution—Plan Time Alone with the Children

There are many ways parents can help children with the transition from a single-parent to a two-parent family. One way is to make sure, especially during the first year, that both parents have some time alone each week with the children. This can be taking a trip to the grocery store, going out to lunch, watching a television show while the other parent is doing something else, or simply going for a walk where they can talk. Any time alone will help children realize that they are still loved and wanted. Private time with the stepparent as well as the biological parent is a good way for the stepparent to become better acquainted with the children. Be careful about insisting that everything be done together.

Problem #3—The "Wicked" Stepparent

Unfortunately, many of the stories that we read to children when they are young depict stepparents as "wicked." When children already predisposed to these thoughts see the stepparent disrupt their lives, many children conclude that the stories were true. Therefore, the stepparent has a very difficult time in the early months, and sometimes years, of the marriage. No matter how hard stepparents try, most children will be unable to instantly love them in the way the stepparent desires. Younger children simply do not have the reasoning power to do more than react to the changes in their environment. Older children may be able to understand things better, but their own wants and desires are still going to come first. While negative words and behavior have more to do with changes brought about by the remarriage than with the stepparent, it is the stepparent who is likely to be blamed.

Suggested Solution—Positive Support from the Biological Parent

In order to counterbalance all the negative images associated with stepparents, the biological parent must use every opportunity to build up the positive things done by the stepparent. The stepparent needs to be openly praised whenever possible. Since children often see the stepparent keeping them from doing many things, when children ask to do something that you know is fine, the biological parent can sometimes say, "I'm not sure that is a good idea, but let me talk to (the stepparent). I'll let you know later." Then when they are told that the stepparent approves the idea, the children begin to see the stepparent in a more positive light. There will be so many times that the stepparent is seen negatively that any opportunity to help children view him or her positively should be used to advantage.

Problem #4—Lack of Respect

One thing that bothers many stepparents is the lack of respect stepchildren may show. Stepchildren often openly defy the stepparent, sometimes totally ignore the stepparent, and frequently refer to the stepparent in the third person as "he" or "she." Some children are more subtle and rebel in ways that are less obvious. They may need to be asked to do something repeatedly; they may neglect to do things the stepparent requests; and they may act as though the stepparent has no say concerning them at all.

Suggested Solution—Family Conferences

While family conferences are sometimes used effectively in nuclear families, in stepfamilies they may be critical. Many stepfamilies have a family conference every week. During these conferences, all family members are allowed to say whatever they want, respectful or not. It is a time to clear the air. If a child wants to say, "I don't like you," this is the time to do it. The stepparent may well respond, "I'm not sure I like you either, but we are going to be living together, and we had better figure out how to do it in a way that we can both accept." In the effective family conference, children are involved in seeking solutions to common problems rather than simply responding (often negatively) to parental dictates. For example, a stepmother can say something like, "I simply cannot live with glasses left all over the house. I know that was all right before, but I just get furious when I see them. I don't think it is my job to put them in the dishwasher, and I can't stand to just leave them where they are. What can we do?" The reply from the children is likely to be, "Don't look at them," and they are probably half serious. However, when they see that they are going to have to find another solution, they probably will. The big difference here is that they are not being told what they must do, but they are being asked to help solve a "living together" problem for the entire family. They will find little advantage in defying a solution in which they played an important part. In time, the children will begin to bring problems of their own that they want the family to help solve.

Problem #5—Family Traditions

Every family has a history. In first marriages, the blending of these histories is relatively simple. After all, there are only two people involved. In subsequent marriages with children, however, there are often a lot more than two people with ideas about how things should be done. Go to a birthday, holiday, or any other celebration involving some tradition within the former family, and someone is sure to say, "But this is the way we've always done it before."

Many stepfamilies fail to take into account the emotional power that traditions have in our lives. Some assume that everyone does things one way—it is simply the way it is done. However, no two families have the same traditions, and the way things are done in one family will certainly differ in some respect from the way they are done in another. In some families, birthdays are almost national holidays; in others, no one makes a fuss. Some open Christmas gifts on Christmas Eve; others insist that nothing be touched until Christmas Day. Some people would never miss fireworks on the Fourth of July; other people could care less. Even the way the toilet paper fits on the roll can create a struggle over "which way is right."

Suggested Solution—Create New Traditions

There is probably no way to address all family traditions before some conflict occurs. However, being aware of the expectations of the various participants (including children) will keep everyone from being surprised about the differences. If one family traditionally celebrates Christmas with a house full of presents for the children, only one gift for the parents, and none for anyone outside the immediate household, while the other family has always given smaller gifts to every member within the extended family, these traditions are going to be difficult to blend. Only by talking about it beforehand can disappointment and potential conflict be avoided.

The easiest way to blend traditions is to start new ones. After talking about how things have been done in the past, the new family can decide how they want to do things now. Sometimes it is a relief to everyone to be able to do things differently— to have a choice and not be locked into "the way it has always been done." As new traditions are developed, stepfamilies usually discover that they have grown closer together, especially if everyone has a say in the development.

Things to Discuss

1. List the names of each of your children. Write beside each name how that child responded to your divorce or the death of his or her parent. Where do you think each child is now in the grief process?

2. From what they have said and the behavior you have observed, how have the individual children responded to your marriage?

3. What changes in living arrangements have occurred during your marriage? Which of the following changes could occur in the future?
   Noncustodial children coming to live with you.
   Children moving to live with the other parent, moving on to college, or out on their own.
   Older children moving back home (for one reason or another).
   Grandchildren coming to reside.

4. What would be your personal response to any of the above changes? What could you do to help the children adjust?

5. What are some of the strong traditions within your previous family? Which of these are in conflict in your present family? What new traditions would you like to establish?

Additional Reading on This Subject

Lewis, Helen Cole, *All About Families the Second Time Around*. Atlanta: Peachtree Publishers, Ltd., 1980. (An excellent book for children.)

Getzoff, Ann, and McClenahan, Carolyn, *Stepkids – A Survival Guide for Teenagers in Stepfamilies*. New York: Walker and Company, 1984. (Great for teenagers AND parents.)

Tickfer, Mildred, *Healing the Hurt — for Teenagers Whose Parents Are Divorced*. Grand Rapids: Baker Book House, 1984. (Chapters 8 and 9 will be especially helpful to teenagers when a parent marries again.)

Chapter 2

Challenges of Stepparenting

One of the most difficult family roles anyone can imagine is that of a stepparent. Almost everyone who becomes one says, "I knew it was going to be difficult, but I didn't know it was going to be this hard." That is probably just as well or no one would take on the task. Being a stepparent is difficult. To say anything less would be to mislead. When one considers the material in the previous chapter about children in stepfamilies, this should hardly be surprising. Remember that for most children, the remarriage of one of their parents is a trauma rather than a celebration. Thus, the stepparent is set up for major conflict from the very start and will likely be blamed for all the bad feelings children encounter in the early years of adjusting to stepfamily life.

Little Time Alone with the Spouse

Upon returning from the honeymoon, if there is one, most stepparents quickly discover that they had more time alone with the person they married prior to the wedding than after it. There seem to be children around all the time. The constant demands of children for attention can be extremely aggravating, especially demands from children with whom one has not bonded. Many stepparents are ready to scream and pull their hair out in less than a month.

Connie and Steve had a wonderful honeymoon in Hawaii. After two weeks in the sun, they felt that they were ready for anything. This was Connie's first marriage but Steve's second. His first wife had died leaving him with three children, ages eleven, eight, and six. When they returned from the honeymoon, Steve's work had backed up enormously, and he spent long hours at the office. When he got home from work, the children were all over him, wanting him to do this and that, asking for his help with homework, and requiring all of his attention. Connie would usually retreat to her room to sew or read a book. She had worked all day, too, and now she wanted some time alone with Steve in the evening. However, she also knew that the children needed him. Therefore, she felt guilty for being jealous. About the only time she saw Steve alone was after the eleven-year-old went to bed at nine thirty. By then, they were usually both too tired to do anything besides watch a television show or go to sleep. Occasionally, her frustration would get the best of her, and they would take this time to argue, mostly over something one of the children had done before he came home.

Connie couldn't believe it. What had she done to herself? She loved Steve tremendously, but they saw more of each other when they were dating than they did now that they lived together. Connie found herself resenting the children, especially the oldest one who would frequently do the exact opposite of what she was told to do, but in whom Steve could see no wrong. The little time they shared alone was soon entirely occupied with arguing about the children. Connie decided that this was ridiculous. "Who needs it?" she asked. "I was happier when I was single." With that, she informed Steve she was leaving.

Steve was dumbfounded. He knew that Connie was having a difficult time with the kids, but surely she wouldn't throw in the towel when they had only been married for two months. They spent the entire night talking. Finally, they agreed to talk with the minister at their church and seek advice about their marriage. Both of them considered their marriage vows to be sacred and did not want to give up on the marriage so soon.

Their minister was a man who very wisely realized that he

did not know much about stepfamilies. However, he did know others who were successfully living in subsequent marriages. Therefore, after listening to them and praying with them, he made arrangements for Connie and Steve to talk with another couple in the church who were in a similar situation.

Rhonda and Michael were that other couple. When they heard Connie and Steve's story, they laughed. "Yes, sounds just like us," said Rhonda. "We came close to splitting three times in that first year. I'm glad now that we didn't, but it was rough."

"What kept you together?" asked Connie.

Rhonda looked at Michael. "I loved him," she said, "and I guess I just wasn't willing to give up. We talked a lot, we argued much, we prayed every day, and we learned how to compromise."

This encounter with another couple who really did understand helped Connie and Steve tremendously. When it was over, Connie agreed to stay, but things were going to be different. If this was going to be a marriage, they needed to spend time together as husband and wife. The children were important, but so were they as a couple. They made plans to have one night alone together each week and an entire weekend alone every other month. They also worked out signals that Connie could give indicating she needed to see Steve alone—immediately.

While this agreement certainly did not solve all of Connie and Steve's problems, it did start them working together on a mutual solution to the difficult task of stepfamily living. Many people in stepfamilies find that time alone together is very hard to arrange. An "instant family" comes with instant struggles. Connie and Steve were wise to seek help, and it was also good that they came to realize that their relationship was important and needed time and attention.

The Outsider

Stepparents often feel like outsiders who do not fit or belong in the new spouse's family. The bond between the biological parent and his or her children is so strong that it can seem impenetrable and uncompromising. In the early months or even years of a new marriage, the stepparent typically tries a variety of approaches in an attempt to be accepted, often to no avail. Finally, the strain can become so unbearable that the stepparent explodes in some fashion, perhaps threatening to leave—to which the children usually remark, "Good!" while the biological parent is horrified. This is a normal progression of events in many stepfamilies, and rather than being a sign of the end, such a blowup is often the very mechanism that brings the family together.

Mack and Ginger had been married two years before such an "explosion" turned their marriage around. Both had been previously divorced, and each brought two children to this marriage. Ginger's thirteen-year-old son and nine-year-old daughter lived with them, while Mack's two sons, ages seventeen and fifteen, lived with their mother.

In a real sense, when Mack and Ginger married, three mini-families came together and tried to live with one another. There were the families of Ginger and her children, of Mack and his children, and of Mack and Ginger as husband and wife. At first, everyone was an outsider in at least one of these families.

Children's feelings have been discussed at length in the previous chapter, and so I will mention here only that children often feel like outsiders in both the relationship between the stepparent and his or her children and in the relationship between the couple. When the children all live together most of the time, after several months of intense squabbling, they frequently become close friends, sometimes even allies, taking sides against the parents. When one set of children resides with the couple on a permanent basis and the other set only lives there periodically, they seldom become very close, often simply tolerating one another. They almost always believe that the stepparent loves his or her "own" children more than the stepchildren, and maybe even more than the spouse.

When there are children on both sides, each partner is likely to feel like an outsider in the relationship of the other partner with his or her children. Spouses can usually sense that their partner has an unconditional love for his or her own children, while at the same time having a very conditional love for them. It is amazing how parents can overlook almost anything a biological child does, while at the same time expecting a spouse and his or her children to behave responsibly. Some of these blind spots are created because what is an "atrocity" in one family may very well have been a "doesn't matter" in the other family. Rarely will any two families come together in perfect harmony. At the same time, the bonding that exists in a biological family frequently allows us to excuse "our own" but not others.

Mack and Ginger each felt like an outsider in their new family. Because Ginger's children lived with them, Mack sensed it more keenly than Ginger. Try as he would, he did not seem to be able to penetrate the wall he felt they had built to keep him out. He tried to be especially nice to Ginger's kids. He took them places, bought them presents, helped them with all kinds of projects, and was very careful not to be critical or demanding. Nothing seemed to make any difference. He still sensed the children's anger and hostility toward him, especially whenever he and Ginger tried to do anything without them. When he could not break into their circle with kindness, he tried force. He demanded that they act differently toward him. They seemed to not even understand what he was saying. Ginger accused him of being unreasonable.

Ginger would often ask the children what they wanted for dinner, but seldom asked Mack. When she did ask him, it was usually after she had asked the kids, and she would say, "Is that all right with you, honey?" Sometimes she would make plans with the children to go to a movie or do something else and then invite Mack to go with them. It seemed to Mack that Ginger and her children had their own little group, with him on the outside tagging along.

It was an increasingly uncomfortable situation. When he tried to express his feeling about it, Ginger replied, "You do the same things with your kids. I don't get upset with you." "But my kids are seldom here," he would say, "and you never want to do the things the boys enjoy."

Neither was quite able to appreciate how the other felt and how being an outsider was keeping them all from becoming a family. "Blending" families is seldom like the portrayal in "The Brady Bunch." The walls around the minifamilies brought together into a stepfamily are very strong and need to be dismantled brick by brick, but they can be thus dismantled only from within. The person on the outside is almost never strong enough to break into the fortress. Only those on the inside can make a doorway for him or her to enter.

The "dismantling" did not begin for Mack and Ginger until they were in their third year together. One night Ginger went into the living room where the kids were watching TV and said, "I didn't have time to make something for dinner. Do you want to go out, or would you rather just order a pizza?" The kids shouted, "Pizza!"

Ginger then went to the dining room where Mack was reading the paper. "Is that all right with you, dear?" she asked.

Although by itself this scene certainly was nothing that should have sparked a major battle, for Mack the feeling of being a second-class citizen in his own home had been building for over two years to the point where he could stand it no longer. On this occasion he exploded. "No it isn't all right with me!" he shouted.

"Well, what do you want then?" asked Ginger, completely taken aback.

"I don't care what we have, but we're not having pizza!" Mack shouted. "And either this group is going to start including me in its plans, or we're not going to BE a family." With that he jumped up from the table, overturning the chair, and stormed off to the bedroom.

It was a turbulent evening for the entire family, but ultimately that outburst made a big difference. Mack finally got their attention. The problem could no longer be ignored, and it became necessary for the family to solve it. Mack and Ginger found great help in a stepfamily support group in their church. They met other couples just like themselves and came to understand that their feelings and frustrations were common. Several of the others had experienced situations almost identical to theirs, and they were able to see how these had been resolved. Mack and Ginger stopped blaming each other, finally working together to create an inclusive family relationship.

The Wicked Stepparent

As mentioned previously, many of the stories people learn as children depict stepparents as being "wicked." Consequently, stepparents begin with a negative image in just about everyone's mind, including their own. While most stepparents endeavor to change this impression, many find that such change is more easily attempted than accomplished.

It is difficult to love children who go out of their way to defy and challenge and who persistently attempt to sabotage the relationship between parent and stepparent. Even when a stepparent understands that children act in this fashion out of a need for stability and continuity, which has nothing to do with the child's real feelings toward the stepparent, somehow that knowledge does not help much in the midst of confrontation.

Most stepparents eventually lose their composure and return to the children the same antagonism the stepparent has received. The children then conclude that the stepparent really is wicked, just as they suspected. Stepparents, who know how hard they tried to be different, feel they were never given a chance. Not every stepfamily follows this pattern, but a great many do. The children tend to blame the stepparent for everything that goes wrong.

Helen and Carter doubted that anything like this would ever happen in their family. It was Helen's first marriage, and she dearly loved Carter's two children from his previous marriage. They were only five and seven, very mannerly, and seemed to love her as much as their father did. Besides, the children lived with their mother most of the time. Helen and Carter would have the children every other weekend, on various holidays, and for a month in the summer. Because she was a schoolteacher, Helen understood children and felt she knew what to expect. She was convinced that Carter's children would never think of her as wicked.

Helen was amazed at how quickly things changed after the wedding. The same children who showed her such affection and devotion before the wedding, became monsters afterwards. One weekend, when she asked them to clean up their room before going home from their visit, they simply ignored her and went out to play. Turning to Carter for support, she found herself even more frustrated when he responded, "It's not so bad. I'll take care of it after they leave. They're only here such a short time. Let them play."

"That's not the point," said Helen. "I asked them to do a

simple little thing, and they openly defied me. We can't let them get away with that."

"Oh, okay," Carter replied. "I guess you're right." With that he went outside, got the kids and brought them back into the house.

They scowled at Helen as they walked by, convinced that their stepmother was a wicked witch after all. While Helen felt terrible, she also believed that the children had to learn to obey her. If that meant being the wicked stepmother, then so be it.

Every family has rules by which it operates. Children learn to obey the rules of society by first learning to obey the rules at home. Helen understood this and believed that good parents put training their children ahead of being liked. Carter believed in such training also, but because he was a biological parent whose children lived with him only periodically, the desire to be liked by his children was especially strong and at times overwhelmed him. One of the real benefits stepparents bring to the home is their objectivity, since their need to be liked by the children is not out of proportion to their sense of propriety.

Of course, one incident never determines long-range feelings and attitudes toward the stepparent. However, given the underlying prejudice against stepparents, it is very difficult for a person not to fall into the many traps along the way that tend to label him or her as wicked. Accepting this as the norm may be the best place to begin, looking forward to the day when these same children will regard the stepparent with respect and perhaps love.

Unappreciated and Ignored

One of the most difficult things stepparents report is being ignored by the stepchildren. Without saying anything nasty, they can cut stepparents to the core by simply ignoring them completely. They will walk into a room, right past the stepparent and talk with the biological parent as though the stepparent was not even there.

Peter often received this treatment from his stepchildren. For a long time he pretended not to notice. He was not going to give the children the satisfaction of knowing they hurt him. He even tried returning it, walking into a room and saying nothing, talking to their mother as though they were not even present, referring to them as "your son" or "your daughter" instead of using their names – all to no avail. They did not seem to care or pay any attention. Finally, when he could take it no longer, Peter called a family meeting.

"I know that you think I've invaded your space," Peter said to the kids, "but like it or not, I'm here to stay. I expect to be acknowledged and recognized. When you see me, I want you to speak to me."

"You don't always speak to us," chimed the children, almost in unison.

"I was just trying to give you back the treatment you gave me," said Peter. "But that is going to change, too. Whenever I see you, I will say hello. I want us to be able to get along. The only way people can live together is by following certain social rules of etiquette. They are like the oil in a car's engine, keeping the moving parts from destroying one another. In the same way, we have been rubbing one another raw. If we are to have a happy home, we are all going to have to add a little "oil" to it. I know that we don't exactly love each other yet, but I hope someday that will happen. In the meantime, let's agree to act with at least a minimum of respect and kindness. I promise to do that with you, and I ask that you do it with me."

The children were somewhat dumbfounded by Peter's speech. They did not seem to know what to say. Finally, his wife, Peggy, who had sat quietly throughout all of this said, "Well, kids?"

"Okay by me," said one.

"Sounds fine to me," said the other.

"Thanks," said Peter. "I appreciate you listening."

While not everything improved immediately, Peter and Peggy talk about that meeting as being like a watershed for them. It was the beginning of their working together as a family. Little by little, the children began involving Peter in things they did. Five years later, it was difficult to remember a time when Peter was shut out.

Victorious

Almost all stepparents who hang in there long enough emerge victorious. It seldom happens quickly, but for those who persevere in the difficult task of stepparenting, there is a great sense of accomplishment. The Stepfamily Association of America says that the average stepfamily will take anywhere from four to seven years to achieve a good working relationship. The process of getting there is often very rough. However, the reward for such labor is worth it. Every stepparent having arrived at this point will say, "I'm glad I did it."

Feeling victorious as a stepparent seldom comes easily. Such a victory is usually fought for inch by inch. Every member of the family must make tremendous adjustments before victory is felt. They must negotiate for time with each other in order that the stepparent, biological parent, and all children will have their needs met. Walls of distrust must be dismantled brick by brick. Fair and impartial rules must be established that enable the family to feel good about living together. And every family member must come to a place where he or she feels appreciated and worthwhile. These are difficult tasks that will never be achieved easily or quickly, but when they are, "victorious" is the only word to describe the feeling.

Jane, a stepmother for ten years, looks back on the early years with disbelief. "I remember them vividly," she says. "Bob's children very intentionally tried to break us up. They admit it. They still wanted Bob and their mother to remarry, and I was in their way. At the time, his relationship with the kids was so fragile that he simply couldn't see what they were doing. They would deliberately defy me and refuse to do something—like putting the dishes away. Then they would tell Bob that they had put them away. At first, he usually believed them rather than me. It was very difficult at the beginning.

"Somehow, in the light of how things are today, it just doesn't seem real. In the first few years, I didn't think that we would even be together today. Bob and I fought all the time, always about his kids. They hated me, and I . . . well, I guess if I'm to be honest, I hated them, too, because of what they did to Bob and me. But now it's hard to describe how close we are. They will come over to the house now, and we will actually laugh at some of the ridiculous things that happened. They told me recently that in those early days when they came to stay for the weekend, they sometimes actually plotted how they could get Bob and me to fight. They feel bad about that now, but at the time, it was a real struggle for all of us."

The love that Bob and I feel for each other is absolutely wonderful. It not only survived those times, it grew immensely through them. We are what we are today, not in spite of our problems, but because of them. As for the children, they're neat kids. They grew through all of this, too. We all did. I guess if I were to give advice to a stepparent, I would say, 'Hang in there. There really is a pot of gold at the end of the rainbow.' "

Things to Discuss

1. What are your hopes and fears about being a stepparent?

2. Of the various topics about stepparents in this chapter— "Little Time Alone with the Spouse," "The Outsider," "The Wicked Stepparent," "Unappreciated and Ignored," and "Victorious"—which do you feel applies most to your situation?

3. What are some things a biological parent can do to help the stepparent and children adjust to one another?

Additional Reading on This Subject

Belovitch, Jeanne, *Making Remarriage Work*. Lexington, Massachusetts: D.C. Heath and Company, 1987. (Chapter 6 is an excellent chapter on "Learning to be a Stepparent.")

Burns, Cherie, *Stepmotherhood*. New York: Harper & Row, 1985.

Somervill, Charles, *Stepfathers*. Louisville: Westminster/John Knox Press, 1989.

Also, be sure to read the chapter in this book on "Helpful Step-family Tools."

Chapter 3

Being a Biological Parent in a Stepfamily

I use the term "biological" parent here rather than "natural," "normal," or "real" parent simply because the opposites of the latter terms have such negative connotations. If one parent is the natural, normal, or real parent, that seems to imply that the stepparent is an unnatural, abnormal, or unreal parent. Since there are so many negative images surrounding stepparents already, we do not need any more.

Most studies of stepfamilies focus on the struggles of the stepparent and the children. Few researchers acknowledge that the role of the biological parent also becomes more difficult and complicated in a stepfamily situation. While it seems that biological parents would have the easiest adjustment to their new role, biological parents often feel like they are in the middle of a tug of war. They spend a considerable amount of time trying to make or keep peace in the family; they juggle their relationship with the spouse and their relationship with the children, trying to keep both from falling apart; and they feel as though they are walking on eggs that could break at any moment. Yes, the role of the biological parent in a stepfamily is every bit as difficult and demanding as the roles of the stepparent and the children.

In the Middle

Most biological parents in stepfamilies soon feel as though they are caught between the relationship with their spouse and the relationship with their children, with both tugging at them and demanding that the biological parent choose sides. The children want to keep the "chummy" relationship they had with Mom or Dad as a single parent. The new spouse wants a primary relationship as husband or wife and a more traditional parental authority in the family. Neither side is wrong in these desires or expectations. However, biological parents get caught in the middle, with children and spouse pulling in opposite directions. Life for the biological parent can be very unpleasant.

Vernon knew this conflict well. His three children, Ginger, Frank, and Matthew, lived with their mother as custodial parent, but Vernon had them one night each week and every other weekend. He had been faithful to his parental commitment with them since the divorce four years earlier. After an initial adjustment following the divorce, Vernon and his children had settled into a pretty good routine, with their relationship deepening over the years. When he married Kathy, Vernon simply assumed that the relationship he had established with his children would now be shared with Kathy. What he discovered was something far different from what he had anticipated.

Vernon and Kathy had dated only four months before they married. While they spent some time together with the children during the time they dated, it was limited because of the visitation schedule. He was usually alone with the children when they stayed with him. When Vernon was seeing his kids, Kathy usually did something with her friends. Consequently, at the time of the marriage, Kathy and the three children did not know one another very well. After Kathy moved in with Vernon, however, all five were thrown together regularly. None of them liked it very much. Ginger, Frank, and Matthew felt like they had lost their dad. "Why do we have to do everything together?" they asked one another, not daring to ask their dad or Kathy. Kathy, who wanted to be included as part of the family now that she had married their dad, felt the animosity of the children and reacted to it. "I don't deserve this kind of treatment," she told Vernon, who replied, "Just give them a little time."

Time, however, did not make things better. The children seemed to resent Kathy's presence more each time they came over, and Kathy, who was now very sensitive to this, bristled at the rudeness they showed her. Vernon, as the biological parent, was caught in the middle. Whenever Kathy was not around, the children would make snide remarks about what she said and did. Vernon tried to stop them, saying things like, "Hey guys, give her a chance. She really is trying to make this work. And didn't you like the supper tonight?"

When he was alone with Kathy, Vernon began to fear what was coming. "Did you see what they did tonight?" Kathy would say. Then she would relate something that one or all of the kids had done that was either against the rules of the house or demonstrated their dislike for her. Vernon thought that she was often being too picky, just waiting and looking for things to go wrong. However, Vernon could not deny that the children did not seem to like Kathy, and he knew that sometimes they deliberately did things to antagonize her.

As time went on, Vernon started to dread the times his children came over to the house – times he used to love. He hated being torn apart by their poor relationship with Kathy. He had a great relationship with his wife when they were alone, and he had an excellent relationship with his children when Kathy was not present, but together, there was tension, struggle, and chaos. Many biological parents experience this tension. When they marry, they assume that the people they love will love one another. What they discover seldom lives up to this fantasy. Love between stepparent and children is not automatic; it takes time, attention, and caring to grow.

Juggler

Biological parents enter a subsequent marriage with hopes and dreams that their new spouse and their children will love one another. When these hopes and dreams go unfulfilled in the early months (or even years) of a subsequent marriage, many biological parents begin to juggle their relationship with spouse and children and see the children without the spouse being present. The biological parent hopes that by keeping spouse and children apart, he or she can promote harmony with everyone. While this is never a satisfying long-term solution, it does seem to provide an escape from the tension. Therefore, the practice of generally seeing the children apart from the spouse is quite common. The problem with doing this is that harmony, love, and the "blending" process are never developed. Tension is temporarily avoided but will always return.

Vernon became a juggler. In one sense, he simply tried to return to the way things were prior to marrying Kathy – a happier time for everyone. He started seeing the children for lunches without Kathy being present. These times were always more relaxed, marked by easy conversation and good humor, and the children and Vernon all had a good time. Most of the time, Vernon did not even tell Kathy that he had seen the children. Also, instead of coming to Vernon's one night each week, the children began coming only every other weekend. When Kathy would go out of town on business, Vernon always saw his children, taking them to a movie, dinner, or the amusement park. Again, to prevent an argument, he usually kept these private times a secret from Kathy. Through all of this, the children seemed happier, Kathy seemed relieved, and Vernon felt less pulled apart. In fact, for a while, Vernon believed that he had found the solution he had been seeking.

The only problem with Vernon's solution was that it prevented the development of any meaningful relationship between the children and Kathy. While they did not have to deal with it as often, now when they were all together, the tension was even worse. By juggling the relationships, Vernon had only succeeded in preventing everyone from coming to grips with the problem. His goal – that one day everyone would be happy together – moved further away from rather than closer to reality.

Vernon began to see the children less and less. Time simply did not allow him to have two separate lives. After playing the juggler for almost a year, Vernon decided to stop the act. He was going to see them together as a family or not at all. When he first announced this, the children rebelled and stayed away for almost two months. However, as he persisted, one by one, they began to come around. It was at this point that Vernon asked for a family conference to discuss how they might work together on a common problem – how they could all enjoy a life together.

The children and Kathy were all very skeptical about this family meeting. Vernon himself dreaded the inevitable confrontation. However, he also hated what his family life had become. Something had to be done.

Vernon began the meeting. "I know no one is very excited about being here right now. Me neither. Frankly, I'm afraid. You see, I love all of you, and it's killing me to see that you dislike each other so much. I just don't know what is going to happen. I'm married to Kathy and I'm committed to this marriage. We're in this for keeps, so somehow you kids are going to have to accept that. And Kathy, they're my kids. I love them – yes, even when they're mean to you. I see what they do, and I don't like it. But I still love them."

Ginger spoke up. "What about what she does to us?"

"When have I ever been mean to you?" asked Kathy, remembering all the times she had had to bite her tongue to keep from saying what she was feeling.

"We know what you think of us," said Ginger. "You may not say it. You just take Dad aside and make him do your dirty work. We know it's not his idea to yell at us. When you're not around, everything is peaceful."

"And when you're not around, everything is fine here too."

"How do you think that makes me feel?" asked Vernon.

"Well, if you would enforce the rules we make," Kathy said to Vernon, "I wouldn't have to take you aside and point out what they did."

"Rules YOU made," said Matthew. "Dad doesn't have any rules."

Vernon ignored Matthew's remark. Instead, he said to Kathy, "Why can't you just tell the kids directly when you are upset. Obviously they know it's from you anyway."

"They're not my kids," said Kathy. "They hate me. Why should they listen to me? Besides, I've tried so hard to get them to like me. I can't tell you how many times I've not said something about things that bothered me. And I've gone out of my way to do things for them, none of which they appreciated."

"Like what?" asked Ginger.

"Remember the blouse I bought for you?" said Kathy. "And the time I mended the dress you ripped so that your mother wouldn't yell at you when you got home? And how many times have I specifically cooked meals that you wanted? Never once did any of you say thank you. Most of the time you criticized the way I fixed them. I really have tried, but now I'm tired of trying."

There were tears in Kathy's eyes, and the children could see that she was really hurt. Even Ginger was surprised; she had concluded that Kathy did not have any feelings.

"Well, maybe you have tried some," said Ginger. "So did we at first, but when you started coming up with all those rules, I think we just decided it wasn't worth it."

"I can't live in a house without any rules," said Kathy. "If everyone does whatever they want, whenever they want to, there will be chaos. Your dad and I live with rules too, you know."

"Like what?" asked Frank, who had been quiet until now.

"Well," said Vernon, seeking to support Kathy, "we have a rule that if either of us is going to get home later than expected, we have to call—just like the rule we gave you. And we have a rule that neither of us is allowed to spend over fifty dollars on something that the other person doesn't know about. Actually, we have developed quite a few rules that make it easier for us to live together."

"It's hard to think of adults having rules," said Matthew.

"I'm afraid that adults have lots of rules to live by," said Kathy. "I have to be at work on time. I have many rules to follow while I'm there. There are a lot of unspoken rules with my own parents, your grandparents. For instance, if I forget to call them every week, they will certainly let me know they expected my call. There are literally thousands of rules that enable people to live with one another. Your rules are no different."

The meeting continued for well over an hour. As it progressed, the tension among them broke. While the situation certainly did not change overnight, that conference was the turning point in their relationship. Once Vernon decided to no longer play the juggler and to work it out, one way or the other, gradually the relationship between Kathy and the children began to change.

Peacemaker

Many biological parents find their role in a stepfamily to be that of peacemaker. Even when the stepparent and children try very hard to make things work, learning to live together is a very difficult task, requiring much patience and love. While the biological parent has that kind of love for both the children and spouse, the stepparent and children seldom have enough of it for each other. Consequently, their nerves begin to rub raw. They start to complain, not to each other but to the biological parent, to the person with whom they all have a loving relationship. Caught in this position, the biological parent usually assumes the role of peacemaker, at least for a time.

Lisa was the custodial parent of two children, Peggy and Jim, ages fourteen and twelve, respectively. While Michael and she were dating, the children adored him. Their biological father lived two thousand miles away, and they actually looked forward to having Michael as a stepfather. After the wedding, when Michael moved in, they began having second thoughts.

Michael could not believe how sloppy the children were. They left their clothes and dirty dishes all over the house, expecting their mother to pick up after them. They seemed to expect the adults in the house to be their domestic servants—at least, that is how it appeared to Michael. One day he simply said to them both, "Don't you kids think it is about time you learned to put your dirty dishes in the dishwasher?"

Peggy and Jim glared at him. While they said nothing, they thought, Whose house does he think this is? And where does he get off telling us what to do? They picked up their dishes and marched to the kitchen. Jim opened the dishwasher and put his dishes inside, but Peggy simply stacked hers in the sink. The battle had begun.

Lisa, who was not present at the time, soon heard about it—from both sides. The children caught her first, almost as soon as she came in the house. "Do you know what Michael did?" they said. "He yelled at us for leaving our dishes in the living room," cried Peggy. "Who does he think he is anyway?"

"Well," said Lisa, "he's your stepfather, and you know, it wouldn't hurt you to help out a little around here. Maybe he shouldn't have yelled at you, but try to get along, will you?"

"We are trying," said Jim.

"Yeah, tell him to try," chimed in Peggy.

A little while later, Lisa found Michael in the den watching the news. "I hear you had a little run-in with the kids," she said.

"All I said was, 'I think it is about time you started putting your dirty dishes away,' " he said.

"And you're right. It is time," said Lisa. "But go easy on them. They haven't had a man around the house for a long time. It will take them a while to adjust."

While Michael tried to be patient, it seemed that the children, especially Peggy, went out of their way to aggravate him. After his comment about the dishes, they seemed to deliberately leave dishes everywhere, just to see if he dared say something. For a while, he simply kept quiet, waiting to see what would happen. He certainly was not going to put them away. Most of the time, Lisa would pick them up. This infuriated Michael, and finally he said to her, "How long are you going to let them get away with such behavior? You know that you are not helping them, don't you? As long as you pick up their things, they will never learn to do it themselves."

"I know," she replied, "but this is a difficult time for them. I'll start making them do more, but let's go slowly. We can't change everything at once."

The next day, Lisa found more dishes in the living room. She called to Peggy and Jim and said, "You two are going to have to start putting your dirty dishes in the dishwasher and not leave them all over the house. We simply can't live this way anymore. I've been easy on you up till now because I knew you were hurting over the divorce and all, but it is time that you begin taking more responsibility around here."

They both looked at her in astonishment. "I bet I know whose idea this is," said Peggy.

"It's my idea, young lady," said Lisa. "Now, pick up those dishes and put them in the dishwasher." "Okay, Mom," they said, and with that they picked up the dishes and took them to the kitchen.

There were many other things that irritated Michael about the children. They were sloppy about their clothes, they tracked mud into the house and never cleaned it up, they never volunteered to help, and they acted like they were being imposed upon if asked to do something. In general, they treated their mother like a slave. While he disliked being the one to always bring up their behavior, he found that he could not keep quiet.

Lisa hated the tension. When she was with Michael, she did her best to calm him down. When she was with the children, she would try to get them to help out more, mostly because she knew that Michael would get angry if they did not. As far as she was concerned, it was easier just to do it herself. She wanted them all to be able to live together in harmony, but that did not seem possible. Lisa wondered if they would be able to continue much longer. While she loved all of them, that did not seem to be enough. The hostilities were escalating almost daily.

Fortunately for Lisa and Michael, there was a chapter of The Stepfamily Association of America in their city. Thinking that they had little to lose, they decided to attend one of the meetings. Both were amazed to discover just how normal they were. It was a great relief to hear "their story" being told by many others and to discover solutions to the problems they had begun to think of as impossible.

Michael heard one man, who was only married a year longer than himself, comment, "You have to choose your battles. You simply can't fight over everything that is wrong. Pick out one or two at a time that really bug you, but let the others go for now. If you don't, it will drive you crazy." "I can do that," thought Michael. "It makes a lot of sense."

Lisa talked with a woman who had been ready to leave her husband because he was always nagging at the children. Lisa asked her, "What did you do that kept you together?"

"We went into counseling," the woman told her, "but the thing that helped most was coming to this group. The people here really do understand. Now we work together on common problems rather than as individuals who see one another as the enemy. We've even gotten the children involved in helping us figure it out."

"How did you do that?" asked Lisa.

"Well, we had a family meeting and asked them what they thought we should do," Lisa was told. "After the children said, 'We think you should get a divorce'—and they were half serious—they came up with some pretty good suggestions that allowed my husband to see that we all could work together on how to live in peace."

"I'm curious," said Lisa. "What did they suggest?"

"Well," the woman said, "our oldest child who was constantly fighting over being able to drive his car to school came up with a plan whereby he could drive to school if he kept a B average in his studies and paid for insurance out of what he earned at his after-school job. We would have been delighted with just the B average, but since he came up with it, we agreed. And you know, he has stuck to it. The other kids came up with a plan to keep their rooms neat in return for being able to stay up later. We compromised on the bedtime hour on school days but did agree to their request for weekends. Everything has run much more smoothly since then."

Being a peacemaker is often the role that biological parents play. They are seldom successful at it for long, but most try to keep the tension between their children and the stepparent from erupting into all-out warfare. At some time during the first two years, the peace usually becomes impossible to maintain, and the stepfamily must move on to another stage that is more to everyone's satisfaction. While the transition is always difficult and often painful, it is a necessary step in stepfamily development, and the sooner it can be made, the better off everyone is.

A New Relationship with Your Children

Both the children and the biological parent usually begin stepfamily living desiring to continue the less-structured and friendly relationship they developed during the time when the biological parent was single. The children and the parent have probably become quite comfortable and satisfied with that easygoing and close relationship. When the biological parent remarries, he or she tries to bring another adult into this circle. However, this almost never works. While the children and the stepparent love the biological parent, they are not nearly that comfortable with each other.

I know of very few adults who, upon coming into a family as outsiders, can quickly find a way into this closed circle around the children and biological parent. While both the biological parent and the children resist the change that accepting another adult into the family demands, the only way a new family relationship can occur is for the biological parent and the children to establish a new relationship. Stephen and his daughters, Marsha and Judy, are good examples. Both were teenagers when Stephen and their mother divorced. After Stephen married his new wife, Sandy, he went through most of the things biological parents experience in stepfamilies. For a while he simply felt pulled apart. Then he tried juggling the relationships. He was constantly trying to make peace and kept praying that the girls and Sandy would begin to like each other.

Of course, none of this happened until Stephen himself forced a change in his own relationship with his daughters. While he could not make Marsha and Judy love their new stepmother, he could reclaim his own position as their father, which is what Stephen did. He told the girls that the family had changed from what it had been when he was a single parent. He could no longer relate to them as though Sandy did not exist. Sandy was his wife and was going to remain his wife. Yes, they were still his children and would always be so. The family was just different from what it had been. It was up to all of them to make that into something good. Stephen told Marsha and Judy that if they were willing to relate to him as a married parent, he was positive they could all be happy. And interestingly, when the change took place in Stephen, the others rapidly followed.

Once this change in relationship is achieved, people often wonder why it was so difficult. Remember, however, change is almost always resisted, even when the results of that change are beneficial. The biological parent must let go, allowing the necessary change to take place. The new relationship that is finally established with the children can be very good for all. While it will certainly be different, different is not bad. Change allows everyone to grow and become something better.

Things to Discuss

1. What hopes and dreams do you have as a biological parent for your stepfamily?

2. What can each of you do to keep the biological parent from being caught in the middle, feeling forced to try and keep peace?

3. What are some battles the stepparent feels need to be fought? Which of these need to be addressed immediately? How can the family win them in a way that nobody loses?

4. How can you help the children adjust to new circumstances without their resenting it?

Additional Reading on This Subject

The biological parent in a stepfamily has been basically ignored in most literature. Hopefully, more will be written about this difficult role in the near future.

Pay particular attention to chapter 5 in this book – "Helpful Stepfamily Tools."

Chapter 4

Outside Relationships That Affect Stepfamilies

When a Former Spouse Has Died

When they marry, many widows and widowers anticipate a marriage similar to the one they had before. However, they quickly discover that their subsequent marriage is greatly different from their first marriage. The new spouse has many ideas, desires, and needs that are different from those of the former spouse. When children are involved, they often have a difficult time accepting the new mate and frequently even resent him or her.

Grief is a slow process. While most people would like to be over it in a few months, it usually takes several years. When it has not been completed prior to a subsequent marriage, it must be continued during that marriage, both for the widow or widower and any children involved.

Of course, many do not allow sufficient time for grief. Just as many divorced persons marry hastily in an attempt to stop the pain, many widowed persons quickly marry again in an effort to re-create something that can never be. While they long for peace and contentment, they must be prepared for hard work and diligent effort. A new spouse needs to be loved for what he or she offers the subsequent marriage as an individual, not as a replacement for someone who has died, nor as a balm to heal a dreadful hurt.

Even two widowed persons who both understand the loss of a spouse will discover just how different a subsequent marriage is from their previous ones. Henry and Cheryl certainly found that to be true. They met at a church meeting about two years after Cheryl's husband had died and just two months after Henry had been widowed. The people at church were delighted with the budding romance that quickly developed, seeing it as a way for both of these lovely people to have happiness in their lives again. That is the way Henry and Cheryl saw it too. None of them understood the complexity of remarriage, nor did they realize that subsequent marriages can also bring disharmony and pain.

They married each other six months after that first encounter. The church was packed. Everyone was very happy for this beautiful couple. Cheryl's teenage daughters were her maid of honor and bridesmaid. Henry's grown son and daughter stood next to him. An astute observer might have been aware that Henry's children were less than enthusiastic about the event, but in the midst of the celebration, no one noticed. On the other hand, Cheryl's children seemed very happy standing next to their mother and had broad smiles throughout the day.

Only after Cheryl and the girls moved into Henry's large house did things begin to come apart. Since Henry's children were now married and on their own, it just seemed logical for his new family to occupy their old space. However, even Henry had not counted on the drastic changes they would want to make. He could tolerate a few of the things the girls wanted to do with their rooms, but somehow he expected the rest of the house to remain the same.

Henry's children were horrified. "Their" rooms looked awful. Both of Henry's children said to their dad, "It's a good thing mother is dead, because this would have killed her." Even their mother's favorite picture had been removed from the living room wall.

Cheryl's daughters, who had been so happy at the wedding, began to have second thoughts about this arrangement almost immediately. When Henry balked about their idea to repaint their rooms and hang up posters of their favorite rock stars, they were furious. Of course, they went to their mother. "Let me talk to him," said Cheryl.

"Why can't they at least hang their posters?" asked Cheryl. "It's in 'their' rooms."

"I just don't like the idea," said Henry. "It cheapens the whole house. Besides, I'm not sure I like the idea of the girls idolizing those people either."

While Henry finally gave in on the posters, this was just the beginning of trouble. Within two months Henry and the girls were in continual conflict, with Cheryl being caught in the middle. Although they sought counseling at the church, the situation did not improve. After being married for only a year and a half, they divorced.

Just because people experience difficulties in remarriage does not mean they will eventually divorce. Even marriages entered into quite hastily are not necessarily doomed to failure. However, there are foreseeable problems. One such problem is that a widow or widower has positive memories of the former spouse that may not be understood or appreciated by the new mate.

Ralph's wife died when he was fifty-five. His children were married and on their own. While he saw them frequently and loved his grandchildren, he felt extremely lonely. He hated going home at night and often found excuses for staying out late. When he met Lois, it seemed like she had been sent to him by God. They had been introduced by a mutual friend who was concerned about them both. Lois's husband had left her after a twenty-five-year marriage, and she was hurting as much as Ralph. Their friend believed that they could take away each other's pain, and they believed that also. They were married four months later.

Problems began almost immediately. When Lois tried to discard all of Ralph's former wife's clothes and erase all evidence of her from their home, Ralph was horrified. While he finally conceded on the issue of the clothes, he balked about several of the other things. "I like the furniture that way," he said. "And why should we give so many things to the children? Mary and I bought those figurines when we were in Germany. They're beautiful, and they are part of my life, too, remember.

It is almost like you are trying to make me forget that I was ever married before."

"But you're married to me now," said Lois. "These things only tend to remind us of the past. We need to put the past away and get on with our lives."

Of course, that was a lot easier said than done. Ralph and Lois spent several shaky years together before they were able to get on with their lives. Grief takes time and is difficult work, whether it is after the death of a mate or after the death of a marriage.

A person marrying someone who has been widowed should not try to compete with the former spouse or try to erase the good memories that continue to exist. The widowed need to be able to talk about the deceased, and although they will usually talk about him or her in very loving ways, it need not diminish or take away from the love felt for a new spouse.

Another unique problem encountered by the widowed when they marry again is where to be buried when they die. They have loving feelings for the former spouse as well as the new spouse. Also, they realize that their children will want Mom and Dad to be buried together. While the divorced who remarry cannot imagine such a thing, this can be a major concern for the widowed (who are very aware of death's reality).

There is certainly no right or wrong answer to this dilemma. Some choose to be buried together and hope that the children will understand. Others choose to be buried with the former spouse for the sake of the children. Still others choose to be cremated and have their ashes scattered in some favorite place. It might be helpful to remember that Jesus said that it would not matter in heaven. In the twelfth chapter of Mark (verses 18-27), Jesus is asked by some Sadducees about a woman who had seven husbands. They wanted to know whose wife she would be in heaven. Jesus told them that in heaven there is no marriage, but that we will be like the angels.

When There Has Been a Divorce

Relationships with former spouses after a divorce range all the way from friendship to out-and-out warfare. While there are probably more who are "at war" than those who remain friends, the majority of divorced people fall somewhere in between. Divorced couples soon learn that divorce does not end the relationship; it only changes the arena. This may not be true if there were no children from the union.

However, if children are involved, parental interaction is going to take place throughout their lives. There is likely to be more involvement during school years when visitation, school activities, child support payments, and the like will be taking place. Nevertheless, there will also be periodic times of involvement after the children are grown – at weddings, health crises and other difficult times, or even the birth of grandchildren. Some continued contact is unavoidable. Learning how to interact with a former spouse in a positive way that will not be threatening to the new spouse is an art that many in subsequent marriages ignore at their peril.

A major advantage of joining a stepfamily support group is the opportunity it provides to talk with people who really do understand about relationships with former spouses and children. Because these past relationships have a way of causing considerable turmoil in the average stepfamily, support groups frequently talk about former spouses. Former spouses are generally considered "bad news," and most couples wish they did not have to interact with them at all.

Depending on which side people find themselves, former spouses either want more money all the time or they never pay the money they owe. They either neglect the kids or they are overindulgent. They almost never understand, they are manipulative, they are immoral, and they are financially irresponsible. Which, of course, is why they are "ex'es." They could not get along together as marrieds. I often have a strange feeling, however, that when our group starts discussing former spouses, there is another group on the other side of the mirror discussing their former spouses in the same way, and we are the former spouses they are talking about.

Andrew and Doris struggled more over his former wife, Marie, than any other problem. It seemed to them that they would have no problems at all if only she had died. They even joked about how great it would be if she simply dropped dead one day. This is a normal feeling and one shared by many divorced persons. Of course, that would only exchange one set of problems for another, since then they would have to deal with the real grief of Andrew's three children, who loved both their mother and father in spite of their parents' behavior toward each other.

Because Andrew and Marie's divorce had not really resolved their differences, they remained combatants, trying to gain after the divorce those things they felt were rightfully theirs but had not been awarded to them by the court. One of the major problems with the legal system is that it creates only winners and losers. Compromise can be achieved only by the efforts of the parties outside of court. Many couples fail to resolve their differences in such a way that each partner feels that he or she can live with the decision. Sometimes, even when the court settlement has been extremely fair, because the emotional distress of one or both parties remains unresolved, fighting after the divorce is almost inevitable. Therefore, they either violate the court decision whenever possible, or they look for an opportunity to go back to court and attempt to get more.

Marie still believed that Andrew had wronged her terribly in seeking the divorce. There was probably no settlement that would have seemed adequate, and one of her goals in life was to make Andrew suffer as much as she had. Therefore, at every opportunity, Marie tried to hurt him and did not hesitate to use the children as weapons. Soon after Andrew and Doris married, Marie took him back to court asking for additional child support since Doris had a good job and no children and they could afford to pay more. The court agreed and raised his payments an extra $100 a month. In return, when Marie sought flexibility from what the court had ordered for weekend visitation, Andrew quickly contacted his attorney and forced her to comply with the visitation as it had been decreed. Of course, Marie did manage frequently to delay things by an hour or so, which to her pleasure infuriated Andrew.

They had been acting like this ever since the divorce, and there seemed to be no end in sight. Worst of all, it was putting such a strain on Andrew and Doris's marriage that they found themselves fighting with each other when it was really Marie they were upset about.

When they sat in my office, telling this totally frustrating story, I could not help but picture three helpless adults and three hurting children caught up in a maze that seemed to have no exit. There are a great many such situations within stepfamilies, but thankfully most have not festered and spread the destruction that this one had.

I knew that I had to get Andrew and Doris to start working as a team to break through this power struggle that was going on with Marie. Such power struggles often follow divorces, with devastating results for both adults and children. Andrew and Doris had to stop focusing their attention on reacting to Marie's every move. They needed to anticipate upcoming events and develop a plan well in advance that would allow them to feel good no matter what Marie did. Once they did this, Marie's actions would no longer be able to throw them for a loop or disrupt their family.

With the Christmas holiday just a month away, this was a good time to see if Andrew and Doris could make such a plan work. "What are the agreed-upon arrangements for Christmas?" I asked. "And what do you think Marie will do to mess things up?"

"We are supposed to pick up the kids at noon on Christmas Day and return them at noon on New Year's Day," they told me. "Last year, however, when we went to get the children, there was a note on the door saying that she had taken the kids to visit her mother, and they would not be back until three o'clock. She said that she had tried to call. However, we had been home all morning and knew that she really hadn't. When I confronted her with that, she said that she must have dialed a wrong number. On top of that, she had bought the kids tickets to the circus the same week that we were supposed to have them, and she gave them the tickets as a Christmas present. She would take them, she told us, but of course that cut into our time and forced us to change our plans for the week. What will she do this year? Something just as bad. You can count on it."

"Okay," I replied. "What can the two of you come up with right now that will put you on the offense instead of the defense? What can you do so that no matter what she does, your plans will not be upset? She only does these things to make you angry. I wonder what would happen if you don't get angry, while at the same time remaining firm about your own plans."

"I don't know," said Andrew. "I suppose it's worth a try. I just don't know how to do it."

"Take last year, for example," I said. "What would have happened if, anticipating that Marie might not be home when you got there on Christmas Day, you had called her in advance, told her specifically that you were going to pick up the children exactly at noon, you were eating dinner at one o'clock, and that you had plans for the entire week."

"I hate talking with her," said Andrew.

"So, you are willing to let her disrupt your life and damage your marriage because you dislike talking with her. Is that what you are saying?" I asked.

"I don't know that it would work, anyway," he replied. "She would probably have given them the circus tickets no matter what I said to her. Then, if I didn't let the kids go, they would have been mad at me."

"If you told her that you already had plans and that she would have to see if she could get her money back, I doubt that it would happen again," I said. "The important thing is for you and Doris to make plans first, letting Marie know what you plan to do rather than waiting to see what she does. She may indeed try to sabotage it, but you will be on the offense rather than the other way around. Be fair. Don't try to hurt her in the process or it will backfire on you, but be proactive rather than reactive. Why don't you and Doris play a game with each other? Try to see who can anticipate exactly what Marie will do. Then, come up with a strategy about how you will counter her every move. Most of all, decide in advance that no matter what she does, you are not going to allow her to upset you or your plans. You are going to enjoy the holiday, no matter what she does."

For the first time, Doris and Andrew began to smile. They began to see some of the possibilities of their taking charge of what had seemed like an impossible situation. I knew that if I could get them to work as a team, no matter what happened, they would win, only growing closer through the tumult. Stepfamilies always win when couples pull together to solve a common problem. It is when they allow the problem to separate them that they lose.

Both biological parents and stepparents experience difficulty sharing children with someone else, having little interaction and certainly no control. It will never be easy and can often hurt for the children to show that they even like this other person. However, for the children's sake, it is important to give them permission to do just that. You do not have to like the other parent or stepparent, but the children will be much better off if you don't stand in the way of this process.

Relationships with former spouses frequently cause strain in subsequent marriages. Every couple must discover how they can relate to this sometimes hostile person in a way that enhances rather than detracts from the family. This may take considerable time and effort. However, if as a couple you learn how to work together on this common problem, it will not pull you apart but will draw you together, strengthening the bond you have with each other.

The Effect of Relatives and Former Relatives on Stepfamilies

When a person has been married before, relationships with relatives from the previous marriage can affect a subsequent marriage. Most widowed persons continue to relate to the relatives of their former spouse as do some divorced persons. Many people feel that these relationships need not be severed simply because there has been a death or a divorce. However, these relationships must not be allowed to interfere with the subsequent marriage.

Let me illustrate. Joe's mother and father stayed in close contact with Joe's former wife, Beth, after their divorce. They had always liked her, and Beth had custody of their three grandchildren. During the three years since the divorce, Joe's parents and Beth saw each other often and frequently did things together. A few years later, Joe married again. While his parents liked Janice and were happy that Joe had met someone he loved, they both still liked Beth more. After all, they had been close to Beth for some eighteen years, and while they had known Janice for over a year, they had not developed a tight bond with her.

This is all very natural, of course, and it would not have been a problem except that whenever Joe's mother was with Janice, she would eventually start talking about Beth and how much she loved her. She would usually add, "Oh, I love you too, you know."

At first, Janice tried to ignore the comments, but as time went on, her mother-in-law's words became more and more irritating. She did not want to hurt Joe's mother, but she did not like being hurt either. Finally, she told Joe that something had to be done. If it happened one more time, she knew that she would end up saying something she might regret.

In this case, Joe went to his mother and talked with her. He told his mother that he respected her relationship with his former wife, Beth, and certainly did not want to interfere with it in any way. However, he loved his present wife, Janice, and would not allow her to be hurt in this way. If his mother needed to talk about Beth, it was going to have to be with someone else. Such conversations were hurting Janice, who was trying to be a loving daughter-in-law. Joe's mother got the message, and the comments ceased.

It may have been that Joe's mother did not even realize that what she was saying hurt Janice, or it may have been that she had not worked out all of her anger over the divorce. Whatever the reason, such situations must not be allowed to fester and create continuing problems for the subsequent marriage. By Joe confronting his mother and dealing with it openly, the family was able to move on. However, parents can often be intimidating, and some people will do just about anything to avoid confronting their parents. Failure to take action when it is called for, even with parents, will only add to the normal struggles of remarriage.

When Charlie and Evelyn married, neither of them anticipated that one of their biggest problems would be Evelyn's former in-laws. Evelyn was a widow whose parents had died when she was young. After she married her first husband, Dan, Evelyn essentially adopted her in-laws as her own parents. Dan's parents were fairly wealthy and helped the young couple over many a hard time in their early years of marriage. When Dan died some thirteen years later, his parents had been an enormous help to Evelyn and her one son, Zachary, both financially and emotionally.

When Evelyn started dating Charlie three years after Dan's death, she could sense a slight distancing in her relationship with Dan's parents. While she certainly did not want to hurt them in any way, her own needs took precedence, and a year later Evelyn and Charlie were married. Dan's parents had been polite enough to Charlie, even attending the wedding and giving them a lovely present. After the wedding, they took Zachary home with them while Evelyn and Charlie went on their honeymoon. Everything seemed as if it was working out, and Evelyn hoped that in time Dan's parents would be able to accept Charlie into their family.

Zachary was fifteen when his mother and Charlie married. He thought that Charlie was all right, but he could see that his grandparents did not care for Charlie very much. In fact, while his mother and new stepfather were away on their honeymoon, his grandparents invited him to come and live with them permanently. They even offered him a new car to drive to school when he turned sixteen, just three months away. Zachary knew that he could get his grandparents to give him anything. In addition, if Zachary lived with the grandparents, he would not have to put up with Charlie's two daughters, ages ten and eight, who were always giggling when they came over. Charlie was divorced, and while the girls lived with their mother, Zachary had been told that the girls would be staying with them two weekends each month and an entire month in the summer. Living with his grandparents seemed like a good idea to Zach.

However, it did not seem like such a good idea to Evelyn. While she loved and respected Dan's parents, she also knew that they were overindulgent with Zach. Besides, she was not about to hand over her parenting responsibilities to others. Zach was her son, and she was going to finish raising him.

When she told Zach he could not live with his grandparents, he became very angry, stormed out of the house, and of course, went to see his grandparents. While they were somewhat caught in the middle, having already extended the offer, they promised to talk with his mother to see if she might not change her mind. Anyway, they assured him that the car would still be his when he turned sixteen.

Evelyn couldn't believe it. Not only had her former husband's parents tried to take her son away from her, now they had promised him a new car for his sixteenth birthday without ever consulting her. When she and Charlie talked about it, they both agreed that having a car of his own would not be good for Zach at this time. However, to tell him and his grandparents that he could not have it was going to create a terrible situation that would obviously develop into a power struggle for Zachary's affection. Both Evelyn and Charlie wanted Zach to love his grandparents, but they simply could not allow the grandparents to interfere with their parental decisions.

Finally, both Evelyn and Charlie went to see her former in-laws. It was not an easy meeting, and several times the situation almost got out of hand. However, when it ended, Dan's parents had agreed to back off, allowing Evelyn to be a functional parent—with their support. Before they gave Zachary anything that cost more than fifty dollars, his grandparents promised they would talk with Evelyn first and get her approval. If they did not do this, they understood that Evelyn and Charlie would refuse to allow them to see their grandson at all. As far as the car was concerned, Zachary would be permitted to have it, but only as long as he obeyed the rules that Evelyn and Charlie set down for driving it.

The first two years within this family were very stormy. Several times Zachary did things to widen the rift between his mother and grandparents. If the grandparents had not been true to their word, the situation would have undoubtedly become much worse. It is questionable whether or not Evelyn and Charlie could have won a power play if one had developed. At age sixteen, Zachary could easily have gone his own way—if the grandparents cooperated. However, their love and concern for the boy helped them understand that Evelyn and Charlie did have Zachary's best interests at heart, and when finally he became a very responsible young man, everyone was able to celebrate.

Not all stepfamily struggles with relatives and former relatives work out this well. Sometimes the relatives refuse to cooperate. Now and then, people feel too intimidated to take action, hoping that the situation will resolve itself. Sometimes the person whose relative is creating the problem thinks that the new spouse, who is usually aware of irritating actions and comments first, is overreacting and should not be so sensitive. Occasionally, these relationships deteriorate to the point of warfare or avoidance.

The important thing to keep in mind in regard to relationships with all relatives is the primacy of the marriage relationship, without which the marriage can never be satisfying. All other relationships must, therefore, be secondary. Since the new mate has no history with other family members, he or she is at a real disadvantage. Family loyalties may very well lie elsewhere – even with the former spouse. It will take time, patience, love, and effort for these relationships to endure and develop. None of this is automatic. Couples who assume that because they love each other, everyone else will love the new mate as well, are setting themselves up for major disappointment.

Things to Discuss

1. (If Divorced) – In what ways does your former spouse still try to manipulate you? How does this make you feel? What do you do about it?

2. (If Widowed) – How would you describe your grief pilgrimage? How far along do you think you are? In what ways is your new mate similar, and different, from your deceased spouse?

3. Which relatives and friends had the most difficulty with your divorce or the death of your spouse? Are any of these having difficulty with your marrying again?

4. If a relative or friend does respond negatively to your new mate, what will you do?

Additional Reading on This Subject

It will be helpful for persons who have not experienced divorce or the death of a mate, yet are marrying someone who has, to read about that experience in order to better understand the person they are marrying. Following are books I think will help.

On the Death of a Spouse

Nudel, Adele Rice, *Starting Over — Help for Young Widows &
Widowers.* New York: Dodd, Mead & Company, Inc., 1986.

On Divorce

Smoke, Jim, *Growing Through Divorce.* Eugene, Oregon: Harvest House Publishers, 1985.

Chapter 5

Helpful
Stepfamily Tools

People struggling with stepfamily living often look for practical tools to use that can help them improve relationships within the family. Over the years, our stepfamily group has developed a few problem-solving approaches that seem to work quite well. Three of these tools are described in this chapter. Learning to use them can ease a lot of tension and aid the stepfamily in its development.

Holding Regular Family Meetings

One technique that has often worked well in stepfamilies is holding regular family meetings. While used successfully in nuclear families as well, family meetings can be almost a necessity in a stepfamily. The family meeting provides a forum for discussing problems where each family member can be heard and where solutions can be worked out.

Joan and Ed believe that family meetings saved their marriage. Joan brought to her new home two children from her previous marriage – Molly, who was ten, and Jeffrey, who was seven. Ed, whose former wife had simply abandoned the family, brought three children to the new family – John, seventeen,

Mike, fifteen, and Julie, twelve. With all seven of them living together, the first year was frequently chaotic. They decided on regular family meetings after only two months of stepfamily living.

The very first meeting set the stage for the ones that followed. As the father, Ed started things off. "This is a lot more difficult than Joan and I thought it would be," he said. "Blending two families is going to take a lot of work. Each of us will need to cooperate, or we will have chaos all the time."

"We already have that," said Julie, Ed's youngest.

"I like it," piped up Jeffrey, the youngest of all.

"Nevertheless," Ed continued, "we need to set down some family rules by which all of us will have to live. We didn't get married to fight all the time. And we're going to have family meetings like this every week. Every Sunday night after dinner we will all come into the living room and talk about whatever is bothering anyone."

"Anything?" asked Molly.

"Yes, anything," said Ed. "This is the place to work things out, no matter what. And since this is a Christian family and we agreed from the beginning that Jesus was going to be our guide, I think we should begin with prayer. We can take turns leading the prayer, but I will lead us tonight.

"Lord, blending two families is a lot harder than I ever imagined. I suspect that each of us feels that way — well, maybe everyone but Jeffrey, anyway."

Although heads were bowed, there were snickers among the children, but they were used to Ed's prayers by now. They knew that he often tried to laugh with God as well as be serious.

"Lord," Ed continued, "we really want to make this home a place where all of us can be happy and where we can grow together. We just don't know exactly how to do it, and we ask for your help. In these family meetings, teach us how to iron out our differences in love, even when we don't feel very loving. Bless our family, dear God, and help us to be a blessing to one another. Amen."

Ed's prayer set the right tone for the first meeting. It is difficult to be angry at people for whom you have just prayed.

Also, it helped the family realize that this was something they were in together. While they might not agree about a lot of things, they could work together to solve common problems, knowing that God was with them.

"Who has something they would like to talk about?" asked Ed. He and Joan had decided upon family meetings because each of them had concerns they wanted to discuss. However, in response to Molly's earlier question about whether or not they could talk about "anything," Ed decided to open the discussion to the children first. Joan and he could bring up their concerns later. This proved to be a wise decision, because in giving the children a chance to talk first, the parents' concerns seemed less demanding.

Molly, Joan's ten-year-old, spoke up quickly. "I do. I want Julie to stop picking on me."

"Then stay out of my room," demanded Julie. "She's always coming into my room and taking my things."

"I do not," said Molly. "I was only in your room one time, and that was because I needed a barrette for my hair."

"You could have asked me first," said Julie.

"You had already gone to school," Molly replied.

"That doesn't make any difference," said Julie. "You went into my room and took my things. Do it again, and I'll break your arm."

"Now, now!" interrupted Joan. "The purpose of these meetings is to talk about problems so that we won't fight all the time. It's important to iron out these differences so that we can get along without breaking arms. You girls have never had a sister before . . . "

"She's not my sister," said Julie, scowling.

"No, and I'm not your mother," replied Joan. "However, we are living together, and we need to figure out how to do that without hurting each other. Julie, what do you think a good rule would be about each other's personal things?"

"I think that everyone should stay out of the other's room and leave their things alone unless they ask first," replied Julie.

"I only did it one time," complained Molly. "And I think she shouldn't be allowed to hit me."

"Okay," said Ed, "we have two possible rules to discuss.

One, that no one goes into another's room or borrows their things without permission; and two, that no one should be allowed to hit anyone. Any discussion about either of these?"

"John and I share a room," said Mike. "It won't work with us."

"Yeah, and we borrow each other's things all the time," added John.

"Well, you two grew up together," said Ed. "I think that makes a difference. How do you think a good rule about rooms and possessions would read, John?"

"Don't ask me," replied John. "This meeting was your idea, not mine. I don't even want to be here. I don't know why we couldn't have just gone on the way we were."

"You mean with all the fighting we were doing?" asked Ed.

"No, I mean before you two got married," said John. "Couldn't you have at least waited until I went away to college?"

"Well, I suppose we could have waited," said Ed, "but then it would have been Mike who was about to leave, and then Julie, and then Molly, and then Jeffrey. Besides, we wanted to have everyone together for a little while at least. I know that it is not easy for you to adjust to all of this, but Joan and I would certainly appreciate it if you would try. You see, we love each other, and we love each of you. We want you to learn to love each other, too, because we plan to be married for a long time. And whether we got married at the right time or the wrong time isn't the question anymore. We are married, and all of us are living together, so we had better figure out how to do it well. Now, has anyone a good idea about what some of these rules should be?"

Joan spoke up. "If John and Mike have an agreement about sharing things, that should be fine, but for the others, I think Julie has a point, and everyone needs to respect other people's property and space. No one should take anything without permission."

"How does that sound?" asked Ed.

"And stay out of their rooms," added Julie.

"Do you agree with that Molly?" asked Ed.

"Okay," said Molly, "but it was only a barrette, and what about her hitting me?"

"Well," said Ed, "I think if punishment is ever needed, it had better come from Joan and myself. After all, we are the parents. Now, Joan and I have a couple of things we would like to discuss." They went on from there to talk about chores that had been assigned to each of the children, bedtime, and cleaning their rooms. There was considerable resistance to some of the rules, especially from John and Mike. They had lived alone with their father and their sister, Julie, for almost two years, during which time there had not been many rules. However, over the next few months, the weekly family meetings helped them smooth out the rough spots, and a solid living arrangement developed that served everyone's needs. Family meetings made a difference.

If the children feel that they have been listened to at family meetings as well as told "how things are going to be," they will usually begin to participate and see the advantage of this family forum. Improvement may take a few weeks or even months, and couples should not get discouraged if the children are unresponsive at first.

On weeks when no one has anything they want to discuss, try playing a game together. A board game, where everyone is sitting and relaxed, can often lead to considerable conversation without the children realizing they are talking. Besides, there is certainly no rule against a family having fun together.

Resisting Instant Answers

Another technique that has proved helpful to many stepfamilies is delaying answers to requests until the couple has had a chance to discuss them in private. Children are very good at asking things from the parent they believe will give them the desired answer. In stepfamilies this is usually the biological parent, but occasionally they will also go to the stepparent. Instant answers often cause friction between the couple, even when the couple is in agreement. Not having been consulted can easily make a partner feel left out. Therefore, many stepfamily couples soon decide never to answer requests from the children until they have had a chance to talk together.

One stepfamily couple that I know also uses this technique with regard to requests from a former spouse. Many of this couple's arguments centered on the husband's former wife. She was constantly calling to ask about various things regarding the children, and he would make a decision based on his best judgment. However, he failed to consider how these decisions affected his present wife, who felt left out and helpless. By saying, "I'll get back to you on that," he was able to discuss the decision with his wife before agreeing to something that affected her as well.

Robert and Shirley were frequently fighting about Robert's feelings that Shirley's children manipulated her, and in doing so manipulated him also. Since they were her biological children, Shirley believed that it was her responsibility to make decisions concerning them. What she failed to consider was that these decisions also affected Robert, who had no say about them. While the arguments usually centered on the actual decision made, the bigger problem was Robert's not being involved.

One day Shirley's two girls caught her after work as she drove into the driveway. "Can we go to the amusement park tonight with Michelle and her parents?" they asked.

Shirley was exhausted from a very busy day at the office. With the girls gone for the evening, she could visualize a pleasant evening at home alone with Robert. Therefore, she said, "I think that would be fine. What time will you be home?"

"The Browns said that we would be back by 11:30," they replied.

"What about dinner?" Shirley asked.

"We're going to get something there," said Kathy, her youngest.

Shirley asked, "How much money will you need?"

"Seven dollars to get in and another five dollars to eat. That's twelve dollars each," replied Susan, her oldest daughter.

Shirley took her wallet from her purse and gave the girls twenty-five dollars. "Have a good time," she told them and watched them hurry along to Michelle's house.

Anticipating a relaxed evening alone with Robert, Shirley was unprepared for his reaction to her decision to let the girls go to the amusement park with the Browns.

"How could you do that without even talking to me?" he shouted. "I was planning on the four of us going to the baseball game at the stadium tonight. They're battling for first place right now. Both of the girls have been saying they want to go sometime. How could you just decide something like this on your own?"

Although Shirley tried to explain to Robert just why she had told the girls they could go to the amusement park without first consulting him, it took them most of the evening to stop arguing.

Consider how the evening could have gone if Shirley had practiced the simple rule of not giving an answer on the spot. When the girls met Shirley as she emerged from her car and asked her about going to the amusement park, Shirley could have said, "Give me a minute to talk it over with Robert, and I'll let you know." After she discovered that Robert had other plans in mind, she could have shared her own desire to have a quiet evening at home alone, just the two of them. Robert might well have said that he still wanted to go to the ball game, but he would probably not have been angry since they were talking about the decision before it was made rather than after the fact. He would probably also have been open to rescheduling the game when it would suit them all.

Most arguments like the one that spoiled the evening for Robert and Shirley are not about the decision that was made. The real problem is being left out of the decision-making process. One way that couples can agree to show real love for one another is to not make decisions before talking with the other partner. While the children will probably complain about this, they will also be learning a good rule about marriage that can be of use to them later on in their lives.

Setting Aside Problem-Solving Time

With all of the struggles of stepfamily living, some couples find that they spend most of their time together talking about problems. Before long, they often wonder why they married and if marriage is worth it. Their marriage seems to be one problem after another, and they have little time for anything else. A useful tool to help keep things in perspective is to postpone discussion of most problems until a prearranged time set aside for just that purpose.

Cathi and Mark started such a practice after they had been

married a little over a year. At that point, their lives had become so chaotic and filled with tension that both of them were
ready to break. During a counseling session, it was suggested
to them that not every problem needed an immediate solution.
Some might better be handled when they were both calm. For
Cathi, that was like turning on a light bulb in her mind, and she
began to see practical applications for how she and Mark could
reclaim some time to enjoy each other and their children.

In the car on the way home from that session, Cathi and
Mark decided to set aside every Saturday morning for just the
two of them to go for a walk where they could talk about any
problems either wanted to discuss. Anything that happened
during the week that did not need an immediate solution would
be postponed until Saturday. They could even make a list of
things they wanted to discuss, but during the week they would
not let everyday problems ruin their time together.

Both Cathi and Mark practiced a time of personal devotions in the morning. Because of different schedules, during the
week each of them read the Bible and their devotional material
separately. Somehow, this had also carried over into the weekends. Now, however, they decided that on Saturdays they would
begin their problem-solving time by reading the Bible and devotional material together, just the two of them, and on Sun-
days the whole family could share such a time before going to
church. Both of them believed that something had to change to
get their lives back on track.

The children living with them, ages eight, ten, and eleven,
were all Cathi's from her previous marriage. Mark had two
grown children in another state whom they saw about once
each year. Cathi informed the children that from nine thirty to
twelve o'clock on Saturday mornings, just the two of them
would be going for a walk. In order that she and Mark would
not have to worry about the children being home alone, she arranged for a teenage neighbor girl to be with them.

"Why can't we come for a walk with you?" asked the children.

"Because this is a time for Mark and I to talk about anything that is troubling us, and we really need to be alone to do
it," she replied.

"Oh boy," said one of the kids. "More rules."

"Perhaps," said Cathi, "but then again, it might give us a chance to let up on a few of the rules. Anyway, we are going to try it for a while, and we need your cooperation. Things have been pretty difficult lately as I'm sure you've noticed. Mark and I think this might help."

While the children were somewhat apprehensive about the idea, each of them had been aware of the tension and were glad their mother and stepfather cared enough to try something. They just did not want any more of Mark's rules.

The Saturday morning walks did make a difference. Everything became more relaxed around the house. During the week, whenever Mark or Cathi encountered something that bothered them, they would say, "I want us to discuss that on our Saturday walk." Sometimes they would write it down on a list just to make sure. Both of them discovered, however, that some of the things that seemed so important earlier in the week had lost much of their steam by Saturday.

The Saturday morning problem-solving time freed Cathi and Mark from constant discussions of family problems. Before they tried the technique of Saturday walks, such talks involved a major amount of time, but now these discussions took place in just a couple of hours. Also, Mark and Cathi were more relaxed with each other and seemed to accomplish more. Even the children noticed the difference and soon easily fell into the routine.

I hope that as you become skilled using these helpful tools – family meetings, joint decision making, and problem-solving time – they will make a difference in your stepfamily. It seems a shame that couples who really love each other should spend much of their time together arguing about family situations rather than enjoying being with one another. Learning to use these valuable tools can help you reclaim that togetherness.

Things to Discuss

1. How much of your time together is spent arguing about the children?

2. Visualize how each of these tools might work for you. Which of them really excites you?

3. How can you involve the children as your allies in this marriage? How might they respond to each of these tools?

Additional Reading on This Subject

Visher, Emily and John, *How to Win as a Stepfamily*, 2nd edition. Chicago: Contemporary Books, Inc., 1982.

Stepfamilies Stepping Ahead, published by The Stepfamily Association of America, 215 Centennial Mall South, Suite 212, Lincoln, Nebraska 68508; 402-477-STEP.

Chapter 6

A Matter of Faith

In 1977 I was divorced. I experienced a tremendous upheaval in all aspects of my life, including my faith. For a while, the church and even God no longer seemed relevant to my present life. It felt like churches belonged exclusively to couples and families; God seemed distant and uncaring. Strangely enough, I found more understanding and support within the secular world than I did within churches. For what seemed like eternity, my faith was a void. I walked through a dark valley of emptiness.

For someone who had lived his whole life within the framework of the church, and for whom faith in God was as natural as breathing, divorce was like moving to a new country with a strange language and no familiar landmarks. I floundered desperately, moving awkwardly from one thing to another, seeking answers and stability. More out of habit than as a matter of faith, I often read the Bible. I wrote out my own thoughts in reaction to what I read. Sometimes I would argue with troublesome passages. Sometimes I became excited with a new idea. Frequently I remained perplexed. One day, reading The Psalms, I discovered just how common the "dark valley" experience is to spiritual growth:

Hear my prayer, O LORD;
  let my cry come to you.
Do not hide your face from me
  in the day of my distress.
I lie awake;
  I am like a lonely bird on the housetop.
My days are like an evening shadow;
  I wither away like grass.
                    —Psalm 102:1-2, 7, 11 (NRSV)

How long, O LORD? Will you forget me forever?
  How long will you hide your face from me?
How long must I bear pain in my soul,
  and have sorrow in my heart all day long?
                    —Psalm 13:1-2 (NRSV)

Like so many others, I learned that faith development often requires a period when a person cannot depend on his or her own resources. Over the next couple of years, I came to where I realized that nothing I did on my own would ease my suffering. Finally, at this lowest point, I cried out for help and found God's open arms waiting for me.

Looking back, it seems like the faith I had known prior to this struggle was as nothing compared to the trust, confidence, and knowledge of God that came thereafter. While I would certainly not care to ever relive the desperation, loneliness, and despair of that time, I could never wish it out of my life either, because I understand how much I needed that experience for my faith to grow.

Struggle Encourages Faith to Grow

Many of you readers have already felt the impact of struggle on your spiritual development. Probably the most exciting thing I experience working with people who go through the tragedy of divorce or the death of a spouse is watching their faith mature. Through the trauma of immense loss, many people come to know God and, more than ever before, trust in God's care. The limitations of self-reliance become evident. The dross of a previous faith burns away in the fire of such struggle, leaving the pure essence of trust, hope, and assurance in a loving God who really does care.

Often at least one person in a subsequent marriage has gone through such a faith struggle. Sometimes they both have. These people enter marriage at a deeper level of personal faith than most people marrying for the first time. Even their selection of a mate is based upon different values than before. While I frequently hear stories of people marrying the same type of person over and over again, my own observation suggests the opposite is true. I see people trying very intentionally not to repeat mistakes of the past, deciding what qualities are important and not important in a spouse, and preparing for marriage far more effectively than they did the first time. On every level, most people in subsequent marriages are more mature than those marrying for the first time.

However, only a few people in subsequent marriages are really prepared for what they experience. While most of the difficult issues are related to the stepfamily itself (and are covered in other sections of this book), others are issues of faith and religion.

Sharing a Faith

Some people in subsequent marriages learned in a previous marriage how important it was for them to be able to share their religious life. For them it was vital to find someone who also wanted to go to church, have family devotions, and pray together. Faye was such a person.

When Faye was growing up, church life had always been important to her. Her family had a daily devotional time, prayed before every meal, and went to church every Sunday. It seemed like the natural thing to do. When she met Bob, she was startled that he did none of these things. While his family were not exactly atheists—they said that they believed in God—they did not attend any church, and religion seemed unimportant to them. Nevertheless, Faye loved Bob very much, and he loved her enough to go to church occasionally. Therefore, she married him.

It was only after the children came and Faye found herself taking them to church alone, that she began to wish that Bob would share this important aspect of her life. The only time he went to church with them was Christmas and Easter, and he only went then because he said he liked the music. While she loved Bob, this was not her idea of how a family should live. She had simply not realized how important her religion was to her as part of the total family life.

It is not surprising, then, that when Bob was killed in a hunting accident after ten years of marriage, Faye vowed never again to marry someone who would not share her faith. A living Christian faith was at the top of her priority list in considering the desirability of those she dated. If she ever did marry again, it would have to be someone who would go to church with her and the children and who would have a devotional life in their home.

Faye's mistake was to imagine that somehow this would take care of everything else. When she met Tom, he seemed to have been sent to her directly from God. He sang in the choir, served on several important committees at the church, was a successful businessman in their community, and believed as she did that religion was important.

Tom was thirty-five, but he had never married. All of Tom's energy had been devoted to his business and his church. He had dated several women in the past, but prior to this, he had simply been too absorbed in his work to give a relationship the time and energy it required. Now, however, things were going well for him, and Tom was ready to settle down.

Tom and Faye attended the same church and had known each other for several years. When her husband died, it seemed like the most natural thing in the world for Faye and Tom to get together. Everyone said that they made a perfect couple. In many ways, they did.

However, Tom had never had children, and he had little understanding of their natural and normal development. After they married, Tom found himself having very little patience and understanding when he was dealing with the kids. He felt that the children were disrespectful to their mother and to him and that they were too often disobedient. When Faye excused their behavior and said that he was overreacting, they both found that even their shared religion could not keep them from quarreling. Sometimes it seemed as if they argued all the time. Even in church, each of them found it difficult not to be angry over something the other had said or done.

Of course, they were both still learning and growing. Faith is never a panacea, solving all our problems without a struggle. Their pastor told them, "Faith is not a 'wonder drug' cure-all or an anesthetic. Faith is the knowledge that God is with us in the struggle, sharing our pain and teaching us to find real solutions." One of the things their pastor recommended was that they see a counselor he knew who had some experience working with stepfamilies. Thus it was that their faith led them into counseling, kept them together, and helped them continue to seek answers long after many others would have given up. While faith in God seldom makes subsequent marriages easier for the individuals involved, it can and does give people the courage and the resources to move ahead.

Unlike Faye, Sylvia determined that if and when she remarried, she did not want a husband who was "too" religious. Her first husband was on so many committees that he seemed to live at the church. He read the Bible all the time, and he was constantly preaching about her many shortcomings. When they finally divorced, Sylvia was relieved to be out from under all of that pressure. Her top priority in a new mate was that he lack religious fervor.

Previous marital experience plays a major role in our choice of a new mate. It can work to our advantage or, unfortunately, to our detriment. Also, the grace of God is of considerable assistance, if we are open to God's guidance. I doubt that Sylvia realized how important her own faith development was to her. She might have repeated Faye's difficult lesson, except that through God's grace she met a man who, while having very strong religious convictions, was also understanding of her own needs. Today they share a religious life on a totally different level than Sylvia had ever realized was possible. She often jokes, "I didn't care if the man I married ever set foot inside the church, but today we're both there more than I could have imagined. I think the difference is that we share it. I am so thankful that God helped me make a better choice than I would have made on my own."

Finding a Church Home

People entering subsequent marriages are usually not as interested in a denomination as they are in finding a church that is accepting of them and in which they can grow in their faith. Sometimes they will have had a negative experience in a particular church and consequently avoid that one, but most couples seem to be very open about seeking a new church home. Often it seems that when people from two diverse backgrounds get married, they look for neutral territory in a denomination they regard as somewhat in between their two previous churches. Also, couples frequently have several denominations represented in their families already, and there seems to be relatively little family pressure these days to remain in one in particular.

As in so many other areas, children often find all of this more difficult than the adults. Frequently church and school are the only constants in their lives. Being expected to change churches is one more upheaval over which they have little or no control, and they are likely to give both parent and stepparent a hard time over it. Even when the children are not strongly attached to a particular church, they may use what attachment they do have as leverage in seeking control, knowing that the biological parent will be very reluctant to make them stop going to a particular church.

Like so many other stepfamily issues, deciding on a church home is something the family should talk about together. While the adults can certainly command the children to obey, children can make any enforced decision very hard to live with. Therefore, adults need to talk openly and clearly about this important decision, explaining why they want to try a particular church and probably settling on a trial period to see how it goes.

The trial period is important because most first visits anywhere are less than satisfactory. It is always difficult to feel comfortable the first few times. Therefore, a trial period of less than a month will not be a very good test for either the children or the adults. Each visit during the trial period can be discussed in a manner that gives everyone the chance to explain what he or she liked or did not like. It is important to explain why something was liked or disliked. "I didn't like it" is not particularly constructive.

Ira and Elaine decided before they married that they would like to find a church home where their whole family could feel comfortable. Both had been active in their respective denominations, but neither felt good about joining the other. Each had two children from a previous marriage. Ira's oldest son, sixteen years old, had lived with him for about a year. His youngest son, age twelve, lived with Ira's former wife. Elaine's one boy, thirteen years old, and her daughter, age ten, both lived with her but visited their father every other weekend.

While both Ira and Elaine wanted the family to go to church together, they realized that none of the children were going to be too happy about this. It had been difficult enough getting them to go to church where they already knew people. Therefore, one weekend when they were all together (something that only occurred about once a month), rather than go out to a movie, they sat and talked. Elaine began. "Ira and I would like us to find a church where we can all go together and feel comfortable," she said. "Going to separate churches is not going to make us feel very close. Tomorrow morning we want to visit a new church. Anybody have a suggestion about which church to try?"

While this may not be a great way to seek a new church home, asking the children for their opinion was brilliant. It helped take the children off the defensive by letting them feel they had some say in the matter. Ira and Elaine were prepared to veto any suggestions of churches where they knew they could not accept certain beliefs.

Julie, Elaine's ten-year-old, spoke first. "I have a friend in school who attends that church over near Grandma's," she said. "We could go there tomorrow."

"Okay," said Elaine. "That's one suggestion. Any others?"

Ira's twelve-year-old, Mike, said, "I'm only here every other weekend. It doesn't matter to me."

"But you're part of this family when you are here," said Elaine. "What you think is important too."

"Well, I'd like to go to the church Mom and I attend," said Mike. "I suppose that's out of the question."

Ira spoke up quickly. "I don't think that's a good idea, Son," he said. "I'm afraid your mother and I would find it very awkward to be in the same church. You can go there on your weekends with her, but I think we will have to find somewhere else to go together."

Joe, Elaine's thirteen-year-old, said, "How about that church at the end of the block? I could ride my skateboard."

"There will be no skateboards on Sunday morning," said Elaine. "But that is a good suggestion. I've thought about us going there too."

"What do you think, Peter?" asked Ira. Peter, Ira's oldest, had been very quiet, which was not characteristic.

"Do whatever you want," said Peter. "I'm going to stay home. I'm too old for that church stuff anyway."

"Not by a long shot, Peter," Ira chided. "Good try, but you know that is not an option. Church is something we do together. Always have and always will. And you're never too old. I don't think I could have made it through the divorce without my faith."

"I don't intend to ever get married," said Peter, "so I guess I won't need it."

"Oh, you'll need it, Peter, whether you marry or not," said Ira. "Anyway, as long as you are living here, we'll go to church as a family. Any suggestions as to where?"

"The church down the block is as good as any, I guess," answered Peter. "Bob from across the street goes there."

"Well," said Ira, "it looks like three have decided on the church down the block. I'll make that four."

"Then we can try the one over by Grandma's the next week," said Julie.

"I think we need to give any church we try a real chance," said Elaine, "unless we all just hate it, that is. Let's give it four weeks and then we can try the one by Grandma's."

"Okay," said Julie, "as long as we try it for four weeks too."

"That's a deal," said Ira.

Nothing will ever take the place of listening to the children's ideas and sharing your own. It is the only way agreement can ever be reached. Parents get into difficulty when they simply tell the children "the way it is going to be." Children are already suspicious of stepparents, and they are bound to resent such action.

Sharing a Faith Makes the Difference

Many people in stepfamilies wonder how couples without a shared faith ever make it. Stepfamily living can be so complicated and stressful that having a unifying force holding them together, urging them to love and forgive, and strengthening their bond as a family can be the most vital aspect of the marriage. Couples who take religion for granted or ignore its importance lose out on a power they will undoubtedly need.

This does not mean that families who go to church together will experience fewer problems than those who do not. The number of problems and struggles will be about the same. However, couples who do not share a faith have only themselves to rely on, while couples with a shared faith know and realize a deeper power. There is something about praying over common problems that really does lead to answers. Even if the struggle is not removed, God is with us in the midst of it. Knowing that we are not alone and being open to God's guidance make all the difference.

Shirley and Fred did not start out with such assistance. Neither of them had gone to church in years, nor were their families very religious. It was just not part of who they were. Church and faith became important to them only when they began to experience problems in their stepfamily and looked for help. The psychologist they visited knew about our stepfamily group and suggested they give it a try as a way of establishing a support system.

Since our stepfamily group is a ministry of our church, it was natural for Fred and Shirley to develop a friendship with several couples from the church. One day, one of these couples asked them, "Where do you attend church?" Our group is very ecumenical, and couples attend from many different churches and denominations.

"Oh, we haven't gone to any church since we married," volunteered Shirley.

"Why not come with us this Sunday?" they asked. "We usually go to nine o'clock worship and to Sunday school at ten thirty. If you like, we can even go to brunch after church."

"Oh, I don't know," said Shirley. "What do you think, Fred?"

"Well, we don't have the kids this weekend," Fred replied. "It might be fun."

Fred, Shirley, and the whole family, have seldom missed a Sunday since then. They have a particular place where they always sit, along with several other stepfamilies. When they tell others this story, it is usually with words like, "We don't know how we ever got along without it. It has made such a difference in our lives. We still have our problems, but they aren't the same. Now we work on problems together and find God to be a big help. We think this church, and the stepfamily group, saved our marriage.

A shared faith does make a difference. Just compare those who have it with those who do not.

Things to Discuss

1. Describe the changes in your faith that have occurred over the years, concentrating on the high points and the low points.

2. How comfortable are you with the church life of your stepfamily? If you could change any part of it, what would you change?

3. How have the children reacted to going to church since your marriage? What is the biggest difficulty concerning the children and church? What are ways to improve the situation?

Supplement
for Persons Preparing
for Remarriage

Chapter 7

When Is a Person Ready to Marry Again?

For many, the answer to the question, When is a person ready to marry again? is as simple as falling in love. They know it when it happens. People look and look for that right person who will make their heart do flips, whereupon they instantly feel ready. Some think they are so ready that they seek marriage with deliberate intention. Classes on such topics as "How to Be Married Within a Year" draw large numbers of people. For many who have been previously married, the single life is awkward; some find adjusting to the world of single living so difficult that they desire to return as rapidly as possible to a lifestyle with which they are more familiar. This, of course, is hardly an indication of actual readiness for marriage, especially if we think in terms of lasting satisfaction rather than just being married.

I know of no one who enters a marriage thinking about the possibility of divorce in the future. Divorce is very painful. Consequently, people marrying again almost never see divorce in their future. Even people who have already been married two or three times plan for this next marriage to last. Wanting a marriage to be successful and making it successful, however, are two different things. Working with thousands of single, and single again, people over the past several years has given me some clues about who is ready and who is not.

Infatuation Is Not a Good Foundation for Marriage

Infatuation and love are often confused. As will be discussed in greater detail later, what feels like love in the early stages of a relationship frequently has more to do with a memory from the prelanguage time of people's infancy than with the person they think they love. While infatuation feels wonderful and may surpass any feeling one has experienced before, it is a seductive illusion that cannot last. Because of its great power, some people seek it over and over again. Disappointed that they are unable to sustain this euphoric feeling in any one relationship, they move from one to another, hoping that the next time will be different.

Consider Bill for example. Bill is what some erroneously call a romantic. He loves being "in love." When he does not have an "in love" relationship in progress, Bill feels lost. His one goal at such times is to seek for and find his new love. All of his nonworking time is spent in places where he might meet that special someone—singles groups, bars, dances, church. It makes little difference to Bill just how or where or who, as long as he meets her. When he does, his entire countenance changes. Suddenly he is in charge of the universe. He and his new love can do anything, conquer any problem, overcome any obstacle. When he is "in love," Bill is also sickeningly happy.

Bill has been married three times. Each time he was sure that this was it; he had found the perfect woman for him, and this time love would last. Inevitably, something always went wrong. Bill would then reason, "I guess she wasn't the right one after all," and the marriage was over. The problem, however, was not Bill, nor was it the women he chose. The reason he could not hold on to the love he sought was because he was pursuing a fantasy, not discovering what real love involved.

Infatuation is not love. That this person seems to be the missing part of oneself is an illusion to which dating couples readily contribute. A woman who actually detests basketball may accept a date to a basketball game with a man she otherwise finds interesting. He, of course, thinks that she likes basketball as much as he does. Surprisingly, she may even begin to enjoy the game simply because she is with him. On the other hand, she is delighted when he accepts her invitation to the symphony. Prior to this time his musical taste never ventured beyond country/western, but he finds that he actually enjoys some of it, although he finds it hard to stay awake through the entire performance. Of course, he does not tell her so because the relationship is still new and he wants her to like him.

These two can quickly move into the early stages of infatuation. Because of the illusion, innocently contributed to by each of the participants, both begin to think of the other person as being very much like themselves. It may even seem that they both like all the same things and want the same things. In the early, intense stages of most relationships, couples hang on every word of the beloved, and thus, they often seem able to anticipate the other person's desires even before expressed. Is it any wonder that they might ask, "Could this be the other half of me?"

The truth, of course, is that each person is an individual with wants, needs, and desires that are sometimes similar to another's, but always different. As the relationship progresses, they begin to know each other better. As they start to relax around each other, the illusion becomes harder to maintain. "Perhaps this other person is not just like me," they fear. "Maybe she does not like the same things or want the same things that I do." Panic sets in, usually sometime between six months and two years. "Could I have been wrong? Is this not the man (or woman) of my dreams? Is this person I thought I loved not a perfect fit, my other half?"

When such thoughts develop, a power struggle usually begins. Each person tries to get the other to conform to the fantasy that still exists in the mind. However, no matter how much a couple may have in common, each of their fantasies is individual and unique. Because their "love" for one another was built upon illusion, at this point in the relationship, they must either go their separate ways or expand their concept of love to include an appreciation of their differences as well as their similarities.

The euphoria of infatuation and its inevitable demise is a cycle that began many years before the couple met. Actually, it began when each of them was born. Studies have shown that in many ways the experience of falling in love is the triggering of a memory from infancy. Babies are unable to distinguish that their caregivers are not simply extensions of themselves. As adults, we are able to recognize that such an idea is nothing more than an illusion. Babies are separate persons, individual and unique. However, none of us begin with that knowledge. Thrust from the womb without any experience, it is natural to see the world around us as tied together, with ourselves at the center. We learn to control these other parts of ourselves in the same way that we learn to control our arms and legs; we just do it differently. To satisfy our hunger, we learn to cry. To get that warm feeling of closeness, we learn to smile and coo. When we are uncomfortable or want to be rocked, we try various techniques until one of them works. It seems that the whole world is at our control, and it is the most powerful time in life – except for one thing. This feeling is an illusion, not reality.

At about age two (they are not called the terrible two's for nothing), children begin to realize that maybe they have made some mistakes in their thinking. They don't always get the response they want from their caregivers. They find out that they have less control over their world than they thought. Sometimes they are even told "no." That is not a word they like to hear. For about a year they fight to bring the world into line with their idea of how they think it should be – or at least, how they want it to be. Finally, they give up and accept the world as it is. Years later, however, deep in their memories there survives a time when they seemed to be at the center of everything and in total control of it.

This is the memory that is triggered when people meet that certain someone and "fall in love." Incidentally, studies also indicate that this chosen person often resembles one of those early caregivers in some way – appearance, voice, or even a scent. But keep in mind – it is a memory, and it is an old memory viewed very imperfectly through the senses of an infant.

With the triggering of that memory, the ancient feelings of power and control return. Here at last is a person who understands and accepts the person in love just as he or she is, a person who likes and dislikes the same things. They think alike! They are in control of the world! There is nothing they cannot do together! No obstacle is too big, no problem is too difficult!

I have had couples come to me to talk about marriage, and as we talked, all I could see were the tremendous struggles that lay ahead for them. Sometimes there were several children from previous marriages. Sometimes there were severe economic problems. Sometimes there were difficulties with former spouses or in-laws that would make even the greatest optimist cringe. Yet, to couples still in the infatuation stage of a relationship, these obstacles seemed like only minor irritations that could be easily overcome.

The period of infatuation is like that. It is a time filled with illusion, and the illusions of infatuation are every bit as false as the illusions of infancy, when we thought we were all-powerful and in total control of the world. Eventually, each must give way to reality. Reality, not infatuation, is the proper foundation for marriage.

Earlier I said that people were in error when they called Bill a romantic. Being enamored with a fantasy is hardly romance. Romance is the sharing of love with a separate and distinct individual. Romance is an affirmative decision people make about how to relate to another person. It can as easily take place twenty years into a relationship as it can at the beginning. Romance is not a fleeting feeling based on a memory from infancy, but upon a love that increases over a period of knowing and appreciating a person as he or she really is.

Whenever I see a couple who are obviously still infatuated with each other, I know that they are not yet ready for marriage. If they marry at this time, the panic and shock of the reality of their separateness may be more than the marriage can bear. It is better to marry a "real" person than it is to marry an illusion.

Taking Responsibility for Your Own Happiness

Another indication that a person is not ready for marriage is when one expects to be made happy by the other person. There is much within today's culture that teaches people that individually they are only "half" people. They are told that they need to find their complementary half in order to be whole.

Songs, romance novels, dating services, and sometimes even the church, contribute to this falsehood. Many people succumb to the lie and think of singleness as simply the time to seek for and find a mate. Without another "half person" to make them whole, they feel that they cannot be complete.

The truth of the matter is that God did not make any half people. Relationships are not like simple addition at all. One half person and another half person do not make a whole anything, unless it is a whole mess. Relationships are more like multiplication: one-half times one-half only equals one-fourth. A good marriage can only be formed by the union of two basically whole people who feel reasonably good about themselves. They are not marrying in order to be okay; they are marrying in order to share their wholeness. Thus, if you take one whole person and multiply it with another whole person, you have a whole relationship—one times one equals one.

Consider Alice for a moment. Alice wanted very much to be married. The first time I met her she told me bluntly, "I don't like being single. I want to be married." A few months later, someone from her singles group asked me, "What do you think of the forthcoming wedding?" I did not need to ask who was getting married; I knew. Not surprisingly, Alice had met a very nice young man who had attended the group for the first time a month before. He was recently divorced with two young children. After their third date, they were engaged. Both thought that they needed to be married in order to be happy. They married, and eight months later they divorced.

The sad part of it all was that, although Alice was attractive, bright, and full of potential, she just could not see herself as whole and complete as a single person. She had bought into the fairy tale that so many people believe in their hearts, namely, that what she needed was to marry her Prince Charming and live happily ever after. After all, that is exactly how all of those wonderful stories end.

While reality may seem more severe, it is simply different. Marriage can be very good for people. When it is done well, it enhances the lives of husband, wife, and any children involved. When there is trust, caring, and good communication, marriage frees people to do a great many creative things with their lives that they would find very difficult to do alone. When a couple and family have moved beyond trying to get the others to do and be something else, and allow others to develop and grow as the unique individuals they are, marriage can be the most enjoyable and rewarding experience of all. When it is bad, of course, marriage is neither enjoyable nor rewarding; it is stifling.

Singleness can also be very fulfilling. It can provide for individual growth that does not depend upon another's permission, approval, or even consultation. Singles can enjoy a variety of freedoms that marrieds often envy. Singles set their own agendas, do things at their own pace, raise children (if any) as they desire, and make their own decisions. Singles sometimes do find it difficult to have fulfilling social experiences, which can and often do require considerable time and effort. However, when a single develops a good network of other single friends, that social life can be a source of great happiness.

I am often amazed at how many singles want to be married and, at the same time, how many marrieds want to be single. People in both groups fail to understand their own responsibility for happiness. It cannot be attained through another *person* any more than it can be found in a particular desired *thing*. Believing that there is a certain person out there somewhere who can make them happy is as erroneous as believing that a certain house, car, job, figure, wardrobe, or other acquisition will fulfill their dreams. While any of these possessions or attributes may be satisfying for a while, genuine fulfillment cannot come from such external sources.

When people begin to accept responsibility for their own happiness and cease to expect it from people or things outside themselves, they are headed in the right direction. Then, if marriage does come, they will be ready. A good marriage requires two people who have already discovered their ability to satisfy their own needs. Only then are they able to give and attend to each other's needs, free of the desperation, possessiveness, and fear that so naturally result from an unhealthy dependence and unrealistic expectations.

Things to Discuss

1. What are several specific things each of you looks forward to in married life?

2. What are three specific things your partner presently does that please you very much? How would you feel if he or she stopped doing those things?

3. What are some things you would simply refuse to do around the house, either because you detest doing them or because you do not see them as being your responsibility?

4. What was your parents' marriage like? What influence has their model had upon you?

5. When you have a difference of opinion, what does each of you do? Who generally gives in? How do you feel after such an encounter?

Additional Reading on This Subject

About Falling in Love

Peck, M. Scott, *The Road Less Traveled.* New York: Simon & Schuster, 1978.

Hine, James R., *The Springtime of Love and Marriage: Guidance for the Early Years of Marriage.* Valley Forge, Pa.: Judson Press, 1985.

Chapter 8

Critical Issues
to Discuss

There is a tendency in marriage for the partners to assume that some problems will just work themselves out. Many couples fall into a pattern of discussing various subjects without reaching an agreement. Each assumes that because there was no hostility, there is no serious conflict. Such assumptions often create problems later. Two particular areas that need to be addressed early on in marriage preparation, and that require periodic reevaluation, are where to live and finances.

Where to Live

Many couples give only brief consideration to the question of where they should live, usually considering only convenience. In subsequent marriages, if both partners have homes, the simplest answer to the question of where to live seems to be for one person to move in with the other. The decisive factors usually are: which home is largest, which house is more strategically located to where they are working, and which home is in the best school district for the children. While these are obvious and important considerations, a couple will quickly discover that the best decision as to where they should live will also be based upon the emotional dynamics of each family member in relation to the others.

For example, take a brief look at Paula and Frank. When they married, Paula was living in the home she had shared with her former husband. It was a large house, conveniently located to where both Paula and Frank worked. Both of Paula's young daughters, Jennifer and Pat, had their own rooms. It would be less disruptive for Paula and her children if Frank, who lived in an apartment, would simply move his things into Paula's home. Frank's one son, Jamey, who would come to live there every other weekend, could occupy Paula's youngest daughter's room, and she could temporarily move in with her sister. The couple had thought this plan through very carefully. Logistically, it should have worked.

What they failed to consider was how each family member would react to the new arrangement. Paula experienced the least difficulty, although it was an adjustment having Frank move into her space, trying to blend his furniture and household items with hers. Frank was easygoing though, and it was not too difficult to convince him to get rid of most of his things and keep hers. After all, they did not need two of everything, and hers were nicer.

Frank felt a little confused. He liked Paula's house, but he did not feel at home there. While he thought that he probably would in time, he found himself always thinking of it as *her* house. Worse yet, it was the home she had shared with her former husband. The furniture, the household items, all of the furnishings were not just *hers*, but *theirs*. Understandably, Frank felt like an outsider who had invaded another's territory. Try as he would, he could not overcome the feeling that he did not belong there. Even after he had worked on the house, adding a garage and porch, the feelings did not subside. He simply felt that he was working on *her* house.

While Jennifer and Pat, Paula's daughters, stayed in their familiar surroundings, their lives were nevertheless disrupted. Frank's living there changed their family structure drastically. Furthermore, they both resented the intrusion when Jamey came for a weekend, forcing them to sacrifice "their" space. "Why can't Jamey just sleep on the couch?" they frequently asked.

Jamey felt the resentment and disliked the whole situation. Nothing he did seemed satisfactory. If he used, or even touched, anything in Pat's room, she was upset. They fought all the time. The weekends he spent with Dad, Paula, and his two stepsisters seemed like a nightmare. When his father lived in the apartment, they did things together, just the two of them. Now, he never saw his father alone anymore. Nothing about this place felt like home to Jamey, and whenever he could, he found a reason not to go.

Not all of these problems were the result of Frank moving into Paula's house. The family would have needed to wrestle with some of these issues no matter where they lived. Nevertheless, what appeared to be a convenient solution only compounded the problems each person had in adjusting to the new family structure. Some of the irritation might have been avoided had the family been able to move into neutral space where everyone made a fresh start together. While this is not always possible, it is always advisable. Where it cannot be done, marrying couples need to anticipate the extra problems and develop a plan of action to deal with each.

Foreseeable Problems and Suggested Solutions

Problem #1:

The person who moves into the other's space will usually feel like an outsider, regardless of other circumstances. Although that feeling will certainly lessen over time, it may never completely disappear. Even if the deed to the house is ultimately listed in both names, the feeling that the original owner is somehow still primary is likely to exist. Furniture, household goods, dishes, cars, and other such things, though sometimes of little actual value and seemingly insignificant, also carry with them a feeling of ownership that only disappears as they are replaced with items the couple purchases together.

Suggested Solution:

If it is not possible to move into neutral space at the beginning of the marriage, set up a timetable for such a move, even though the move may be five years in the future. With a common goal to work toward, the entire family can start to make plans about where they would like to live and the type of house they would enjoy. Since the feeling of ownership in the present house will then be something temporary, everyone can relax and look forward to the time when things will change. The family can always reevaluate the plan before taking action. Who knows? They may even decide that they want to stay right where they are. However, they need to be ready to move if their choice of living space threatens marital happiness. It is better to sacrifice a house to the marriage than the other way around.

Problem #2:

If the house was shared with a former spouse who is deceased, that person's presence will still be noticed. The person moving in will probably have great difficulty because he or she has not had time to adjust to this situation. The person moving in may even feel somewhat threatened by the unseen person. Houses where someone has died usually contain several "shrines" to that person, some of which are not intended and not even suspected by the people living there until the newcomer tries to make a change. Let a new spouse try to move a certain picture, or even a piece of furniture, and they are likely to hear something like, "But that is where Mom always kept it. You can't move that."

Some of these same problems will exist where the house has been shared with a divorced spouse, especially for the children. The children will be very suspicious of any changes that are made, and they will blame all changes on the stepparent. "After all," they will reason, "if it weren't for _____, none of this would be happening. Things were better the way they were."

Suggested Solution:

Neutral territory is particularly important in these situations. While children will probably resent having to move, only in a different setting will families be able to allow for all the changes brought about by a new spouse and, thus, begin to grow as a new family unit. If the couple must reside, even temporarily, in a house that was shared by one partner and a former spouse, the persons moving in need to be aware that the inevitable changes are likely to upset certain family members. Therefore, it is critical that the entire family spend time discussing possible changes before they take place, rather than arguing about them later. Children need to be included in these conversations, and they need to believe they have been heard and not simply told about what is to happen. If they do not feel a part of the changes, they will certainly sabotage these and all future changes whenever possible in an effort to feel they are not completely powerless to control their situation.

Things to Discuss

1. How does each of you feel about where you will be living after you marry? How was the decision made? Is this the best possible choice or is there something else you would prefer?

2. What arrangements have been made for the children who will be living with you? Have you talked with them? How supportive are they of this plan?

3. Are there noncustodial children who will be living with you from time to time? Where will they stay? What are their thoughts about this? Where would they stay if they chose to (and you agreed for them to) live there permanently?

4. If there are older children, is there a place for them to return on occasion? How would each of you respond if this were to happen?

Finances

Finances are a frequent trouble spot in all marriages. In a subsequent marriage, financial matters are often more complicated than they are in a first marriage. However, since finances are thought to be very personal, many couples fail to discuss how their money should be handled until after they marry. The circumstances of day-to-day living and paying monthly bills usually force a couple to develop some plan of action. While there is no one "right" way, it is imperative that every couple form a plan that will work for and protect them. A certain amount of financial planning prior to the wedding will prevent the need for a "crisis plan" later, when working out a financial agreement is likely to be more difficult.

The time of singleness prior to remarriage often makes people of both sexes very independent. They become accustomed to controlling their own finances and frequently do not feel comfortable relinquishing that control. Consider Mary and John, for example. Each of them had been divorced for over five years. Mary had a good job and her own house, furniture, and automobile. She had successfully managed her own finances for a long time. John had done the same. Both remembered previous marriages in which they had little control over finances, and neither wanted to relinquish that part of being independent. Mary had a son who was putting himself through college; John had a daughter in college and a son who was a sophomore in high school. In addition to the financial obligations to his children, John had an accumulation of debt related to the loss of one business and the start of another. While finances were steadily improving for John, he did not want Mary to assume any of his obligations, nor was Mary so inclined.

When they married, Mary and John simply continued to keep all of their finances separate. Each maintained a separate checking account, and Mary had a small savings account to which she contributed regularly. Each month, they would total the household expenses, including the mortgage, maintenance, utilities, food, and insurance. They divided the cost in half, and each contributed that amount to a third joint checking account from which these bills were paid. John took care of his own obligations from what he had remaining, and Mary did the same.

In contrast, Paul and Barbara wanted to begin their marriage with everything together. Each brought similar assets to the union, and it seemed only right that they begin with both a joint checking account and a joint savings account. Each month they would both put their paychecks into these accounts, keeping similar amounts for personal use. They paid their bills together. For them, keeping their finances together and paying bills together made them feel more like partners. While Paul did have a daughter from a previous marriage, she was already married and caused no financial obligation. Barbara had one teenage daughter who lived with them and for whom she received child support, which also went into the joint account. This arrangement worked well for them.

The way each couple handles finances is in no small way related to their family circumstances. In stepfamilies, many different factors may be involved. Some of these are:

The similarity or difference between the separate incomes of the husband and wife.

The number, age, and actual expenses related to any custodial and noncustodial children.

Alimony and child support paid or received.

Past indebtedness or accumulated wealth.

Anticipated obligations for college expenses.

History of how finances were handled or mishandled in the previous marriage.

Apprehension about what could happen to each partner's finances if this marriage fails.

Desire to leave an inheritance to one's biological children.

For these reasons, and probably more, some couples in subsequent marriages do not completely integrate their finances for years. The emotional struggles over such a move are every bit as complicated as the circumstances surrounding subsequent marriages. Couples preparing to marry again must evaluate their situation and develop a plan that will work for them. Their plan will need to be examined and reexamined for several years, until a financial plan is reached that is satisfactory for both.

Foreseeable Problems and Suggested Solutions

Problem #1:

One person may want to keep separate accounts while the other wants to put everything together. People wanting separate financial accounts may fear the loss of control that a joint account would bring. For whatever reason, whether arising out of previous marriage experiences or simply the autonomy of single living, they are not comfortable with having everything together. Such people want control of their own money, which does not mean that they are unwilling to share or work to-

gether. They are simply apprehensive of what a joint account
could mean for them personally. People wanting all financial
accounts in common often see this as a matter of commitment.
They often fear that the other person's desire for separate accounts means a lack of commitment to the marriage. They have
a difficult time comprehending the other person's anxiety since
it is unlike their own experience and feeling. Thus an impasse is
reached that may be difficult to move beyond.

Suggested Solution:

A couple trying to integrate financial matters should begin
by seeking to understand the emotional struggle within each
partner. The struggle may be slight or it may be extensive. A
couple will only discover the extent of their differences by discussing the matter openly and without passing judgment on
each other's preferences. If one person is feeling very anxious
about finances, open and objective discussion may be difficult.
Sometimes the person most reluctant about putting everything together will prevail simply because there is unlikely to
be a wedding any other way. Nevertheless, the integration of
finances can remain an ultimate goal that can be reconsidered
periodically throughout the marriage as circumstances change.
I have known couples who began their marriage with several
separate accounts. Years later, the separate accounts simply
did not make sense. Therefore, they opened joint accounts,
both to pay bills and to save for the future. I have known other
couples who still had separate accounts ten years after they
were married. Each couple must decide what will work for
them.

Problem #2:

Achieving fairness is a tricky endeavor in stepfamilies.
When there are children on both sides from previous marriages,
couples often strive very hard to be fair to all, especially when
it comes to allocating the family's money. If Sandra buys her
biological daughter a new dress, she may feel the need to get
something for Matthew's son also, whether he needs it or not.
While nuclear families often experience this struggle, and while
the children will certainly fuel the fires of guilt with statements
like "What did you buy for ME?" the fragile nature of most

stepfamilies causes many parents to stretch the matter of fairness to its outer extremities.

Suggested Solution:

If a couple can discuss the financial needs of each child as the needs arise and avoid the biological parent or the stepparent being caught between spouse and child, the couple will be better able to make sensible financial decisions concerning the children. Good decisions are based upon reason, not emotion. While it will be difficult at first, with practice the couple can make it happen. The secret is to be aware of your own emotions, share them privately with your spouse, and remain flexible. In your conversations, avoid blame and judgment. Use statements like "I am having a difficult time with buying a new dress for Stacy. She needs it, but if I do, I know that Peter will ask what I bought for him. He doesn't need anything right now, but I want to be fair. What should I do?" By approaching the issue in this manner, most couples will find that they are able to avoid some of the emotional traps of the fairness issue.

Things to Discuss

1. What monthly income will each of you be bringing to the family?

2. Will there be child support income received? How much? What has been the history of such payments?

3. What are the expenses anticipated each month? Your list should include at a minimum:

   housing (rent or mortgage, maintenance, taxes, insurance)
   food and other household expenses
   utilities
   automobiles (payments, maintenance, repairs, gasoline, insurance)
   alimony and child support payments
   church and other charities
   consumer debts
   clothing
   life and health insurance

entertainment
savings
vacation
other

4. How will the monthly expenses be paid? By whom? From what income?

5. Will there be joint checking and savings accounts, or will each of you maintain separate accounts?

Additional Reading on This Subject

Estess, Patricia Schiff, *Remarriage and Your Money*. Boston: Little, Brown and Company, 1992. (An excellent book covering a wide array of topics related to stepfamilies and money.)

Chapter 9

Prenuptial Agreements and Wills

Prenuptial Agreements

In most subsequent marriages, the persons marrying have a greater number of tangible possessions than in first marriages. If either has been previously divorced, that person may be concerned about what will happen if such a thing were to occur again. This does not necessarily mean that they are not committed to the marriage. However, they have experienced the pain of divorce before, and they have experienced the legal ramifications of it as well. They are cautious.

Consequently, some couples choose to draw up a legal contract prior to the wedding. The contract is called a prenuptial, antenuptial, or premarital agreement. In this contract, they agree beforehand just how their respective possessions will be divided in the event of a future divorce. Some may think it strange to talk about the possibility of divorce even before marrying, and some may feel that taking such an action shows a lack of commitment. However, for many who have had a bad divorce experience, drawing up such an agreement is the only way they will ever consider remarriage.

Take the case of Harry and Joyce. Both had been divorced

after marriages of several years. Each had children from their previous marriages. Harry owned a car dealership that he wanted to someday turn over to his son Greg, who already worked there part-time. After his divorce, Harry had paid a large settlement to his former wife for her share of the business. While he hoped to be married to Joyce for the remainder of his life, lifelong marriage had also been his intention before, and Harry knew that sometimes hopes and intentions are not fulfilled. He felt that he had to protect himself and Greg, and he wanted a prenuptial agreement so that the car dealership would remain his alone.

Joyce's parents had recently died, leaving her a sizable inheritance. She did not believe that Harry and his son should have any claim on her parents' estate in the event that something would go wrong with this marriage. Her brother was especially insistent, telling her that it was her obligation to protect the future of her two grown children from the financial risks of Harry's business. She realized that, in spite of their best intentions, relationships can fall apart, and she had also learned that she did not have total control over such things. Joyce wanted the inheritance she brought to the marriage to remain hers alone.

For Harry and Joyce, a prenuptial agreement gave them both the protection they felt they needed in order to marry again, and it also relieved the apprehensions of both their families. What they accumulated during their years together would be common property; what they brought to the marriage would remain separate. As it turned out, Harry's son went on to college and became a teacher. Joyce, in time, became interested in the car business, investing some of her inheritance into enlarging it. After eight years of marriage, their finances were so intertwined that they dissolved the prenuptial agreement that had been so important to them when they married.

Many situations are not that simple. Much of the time there is an imbalance of possessions brought to the marriage, with one person wanting the security of an agreement and the other person feeling vulnerable and helpless. Also, prenuptials are not without emotional strain. George and Cindy discovered this when they decided to draw up one before their wedding. George had his own business and a large stock portfolio that he wanted to protect, "just in case." He also had four children from a previous marriage that he felt deserved to inherit the bulk of his estate. Cindy had never been married before. She agreed to the idea of such a contract, but she did see an attorney for advice since she wanted some protection for any children she and George might have together. In the process of drawing up the prenuptial agreement, Cindy discovered that George had been less than honest about the value of his holdings, which were much more extensive than she had been led to believe. Also, George said that he did not want any more children and seemed unwilling to yield much in terms of her needs if the marriage did dissolve. His attitude was that she brought nothing into the marriage, and that she should take nothing out of it if things did not work. The more they struggled over the agreement, the more they began to dislike each other. Ultimately, the marriage was called off, each going separate ways.

People entering subsequent marriages may also be concerned about inadvertently assuming the prior debts of a future partner. A prenuptial agreement is one way to protect against that. Divorce can have devastating financial results for everyone involved. Therefore, a person marrying again may have less than a good credit history, and sometimes he or she may have enormous debt.

Heather had been extremely frugal after her divorce. Debts had always troubled her, and she would do without rather than not pay them. Not only did she always live within her budget, part of that budget was her savings for any emergency that might arise. Gary, on the other hand, was more concerned with satisfying his immediate desires than with always paying his bills on time. He did not worry much about debt, was about $3,000 behind in child support, had a bad credit rating, and owed about $8,500 in back taxes, which the IRS was trying to collect.

Although she was very much in love with him, Heather was apprehensive about marrying Gary because she knew that when she did, her own good credit rating would be at risk. While they agreed that in their new home Heather would manage the money, she did not want to assume Gary's debts, and she was afraid of what might happen to her own finances if the marriage did break up at a future date. She wanted to know what her liability might be and if there was a way to protect herself. An attorney friend suggested to her the possibility of a prenuptial agreement. Through such an agreement before the marriage, Gary's prior debt was his own responsibility, and Heather was able to keep her own credit separate from her husband's.

Debt and poor credit are real pitfalls for subsequent marriages. Without the protection of a legal agreement, a person with excellent credit and no significant debt can be financially ruined in the event of a later divorce. Even if they keep their finances completely separate, in the event of divorce, each spouse may be responsible for half of any outstanding debt, and poor management by one spouse can adversely affect the credit of both.

Since a prenuptial agreement is a legal contract, attorneys are generally involved. While couples often try to do this with only one lawyer, the man and woman will have certain conflicting interests, and no attorney can ethically represent clients on both sides. A single attorney may draw up such a contract, but must make it clear that the attorney represents only one side. If the other person signs such an agreement, he or she does so without benefit of legal representation. If people do hire a second lawyer in order to represent their best interests, the attorneys will probably try to negotiate better positions for their respective clients. Thus, although negotiations can become rather heated, the result will be more fair to both sides.

While the validity of prenuptial agreements of some type is now recognized in every state, the laws concerning them vary. What may be enforceable in one state may not be enforceable in another. Couples moving from one state to another may find that an agreement reached prior to marrying is not valid in their new state of residence. In every state, a prenuptial agreement is not valid unless it satisfies three minimum requirements: (1) voluntary acceptance of the agreement with knowledge of its content; (2) no duress or fraud in the negotiation; and (3) full and complete disclosure of the financial status of each spouse. Even if the minimum requirements are met, either party may challenge the agreement in court if the marriage is dissolved.

Whether or not a prenuptial agreement is made, making a

list of financial assets that each brings to the union is of considerable value to the marriage. Just as it is important to discuss how finances will be handled in the new family, it is also valuable to talk about what will happen to the assets and debts that formerly were the property or obligation of only one. There may also be additional concerns about financial protection for one's biological children and even stepchildren.

Things to Discuss

1. What are the financial assets and liabilities of each? Your list should include as a minimum:

   ASSETS
   houses and property
   business assets
   child support and alimony received
   checking account balances
   savings account balances
   stocks and bonds
   retirement plans
   life insurance

   LIABILITIES
   mortgage payments
   consumer debts
   personal debts
   child support and alimony payments

2. What concerns do you have about finances as you enter this marriage?

3. How do you want your children protected if something were to happen to this marriage?

Wills

While most couples will probably not make a prenuptial agreement, every couple entering a subsequent marriage needs to make wills. There is simply no way to ensure that an estate will be divided as you would desire apart from the making of wills. Keep in mind that each state has already decided how your property will be divided in the event that one or both of you should die without a will. The property of one who dies without a will must be divided according to that state's intestacy laws. Also, keep in mind that the state's division of your property will probably not protect the interests of your family in the specific ways that you would like. Intestacy laws generally divide property according to marriage and blood relationship to the deceased. While these laws would apply to all families, they are particularly significant for stepfamilies in which one or both spouses have children from a previous marriage.

Alice and Bob had talked about making wills before they married, but with all of the things to do prior to a wedding, time had slipped by and they never did it. After they were married, it was one of those things that they continually put off doing. Each of them had two children from previous marriages. Bob's children were both teenagers who lived with his former spouse, who had also remarried. He paid child support for them and felt obligated to help them through college. He loved his children and certainly wanted to leave them something at the time of his death. Alice's two children were very young when they married, being virtually abandoned by the biological father, who did not interact with them at all and who paid no support. Since the children were so young when Alice and Bob married, Alice gave up her outside employment to stay home and raise them. During their eight years together, Bob developed his own business. Most of the family assets were poured into that business. Things were progressing nicely, and both Alice and Bob looked forward to the day when the children would be grown, allowing them the freedom to enjoy the profits of their labor. However, this was not to be. Unexpectedly, Bob died in an accident, leaving no valid will. Under the intestacy laws of the state where they lived, Alice was entitled to only one-third of Bob's estate. The other two-thirds went to Bob's children from his previous marriage. Alice was forced to sell the business and even the family home in order to pay this obligation. Alice and her children then moved into an inexpensive apartment, and she went back to work at an entry-level job position.

This was certainly not what Bob had in mind for Alice and her children, but it is the kind of thing that can happen when a couple has not taken the time and effort to draw up valid wills when they enter into a subsequent marriage. Every couple needs to take the fragileness of life seriously, providing for each other and their children in the event of an untimely death.

Wills also need to be updated periodically. A family with small children faces different financial challenges than a family with college-age or married children. Therefore, wills need to be read over from time to time, to make sure that the dispositions are still desirable. In some states, an old will may no longer be valid. For example, in Georgia (where I live), a will becomes invalid if there is a marriage, divorce, birth, or adoption, unless the will mentions that it is made in contemplation of such events.

Couples will save themselves time and money if they are prepared before consulting an attorney. As well as knowing how they want their property divided, they need to take with them:

1. a list of all property;
2. photocopies of documents relating to property ownership;
3. life insurance information;
4. savings and checking account information;
5. full names, birth dates, and relationships of people they want as beneficiaries;
6. an accurate description or photographs of any family heirlooms they want to give to specific persons.

Unlike prenuptial agreements, wills usually pose no ethical conflict between the interests of persons marrying again. Therefore, one attorney can, and usually does, prepare wills for both people. Aside from cost effectiveness, the advantage of having one attorney prepare both wills is that the wills are more likely to provide a comprehensive family plan. Both persons should participate in the will consultations, especially in the beginning. While each will may "mirror" the provisions of the other, each individual needs to have his or her own will that provides for the disposition of his or her own property.

It is never pleasant to think about one or both persons dying. It is even more unpleasant to think about this when you are planning a wedding. However, failure to do so will create a nagging fear that you have not adequately protected your family in the event of death. The making of wills frees you to get on to more enjoyable things, knowing that if something were to happen, at least your desires could be followed. Just a few hours of what many would regard as unpleasant work can purchase considerable peace of mind.

Things to Discuss

1. What property does each own, and what should happen to it in the event of that person's death?

2. Who should inherit any other assets?

3. What financial problems would the survivor face if one spouse died unexpectedly? To what extent could these be minimized by life insurance?

4. What would you like to happen with any family heirlooms?

Chapter 10

The Wedding

Weddings can be fun. For those marrying again, they usually are. People who have been married before have a different sense about what is important in a wedding. They are less interested in show, and they are more concerned about the ceremony expressing their love for each other in an intimate setting with close friends. People marrying again are often more creative, and they are less dependent upon what others have done than those marrying for the first time. Being older and more mature, people marrying again are more likely to do what they want, rather than what family or friends have told them to do. Remarriage weddings range all the way from a traditional wedding at the church to a private ceremony at home.

Those marrying again generally pay for their wedding themselves and are generally more frugal, spending less on the wedding itself than do people marrying for the first time. This may be because weddings for first marriages are often paid for by parents or because previously married individuals may have more financial responsibilities. Consequently, they are more price conscious. Unless the couple has an abundance of money, they will probably have a small ceremony, either at the church or at their home, and a party-like reception following.

About half the weddings I perform for people entering subsequent marriages are in homes, either their own or one borrowed from a friend or family member for the occasion. I have come to regard home ceremonies to be as appropriate as church weddings. Weddings at home are often more relaxed and intimate than those performed at church. Also, they are very cost efficient, with no fees required for the use of a building, custodian, organist, and so forth. There is something very personal about family and friends standing around a couple in a living room as they declare their love and commitment to each other. Theologically, it reminds us that God is with us in our homes as well as at the church.

Let me share some of my experiences with a few of the more unique weddings held for couples in subsequent marriages. One couple, struggling with finances, borrowed the home of a friend. They held the ceremony outside beside a stream running through the property. Their friends simply stood around them while they said their vows and exchanged rings. After the ceremony, a reception was held that consisted of food the guests had brought. No one attending this wedding seemed the least put out that they were invited to come and bring a dish of food to share with the other guests. In fact, it was one of the most joyful and warm weddings I have ever attended. We refer to it as the "covered dish" wedding.

Another couple held their wedding at a small retreat center near where they lived. Since guests were arriving from various distances, they held a small welcoming reception as the guests arrived. When everyone expected was there, they simply moved into the small chapel and held the ceremony. Such informality could never have happened in most church settings. The reception that followed consisted of food prepared by the bride's family.

A third couple, also watching their budget, wanted a church wedding but did not feel they could afford a reception for very many people. As part of the ceremony in the church, they invited their friends to gather around the altar area, completely encircling the wedding party for a prayer and a blessing. Following the ceremony, they invited the guests to join them at a dance hall where they had met. Almost all of the guests went, with each being responsible for any food or drink ordered. A cake was furnished by friends, but other than that, people were on their own. Needless to say, everyone had a great time.

Another couple invited only family to the ceremony at the church. Rather than sitting in the pews, the family stood around the couple at the altar. The groom's two grown daughters stood beside him, and the bride's three-year-old daughter did what most three-year-olds do: She went from one person to another. The setting was so informal, however, that her movements and even talking were not disruptive. Following the ceremony, about a hundred people gathered at the bride's parents' home for a lovely catered reception.

These are a few examples of how some couples have had lovely weddings without spending much money. Where economy is not a high priority, couples may well prefer to be more traditional. The important thing at any wedding is for the couple to publicly express their love and commitment in a manner consistent with their faith. There are a variety of ways this can be done, and couples must choose what is best for them.

The Children

Every stepfamily wedding involves at least one person who has a child, or children, from a previous marriage. Many couples wonder about whether or not to include the children in the wedding, and if they do so, how can it be done? It is my opinion that children need to be invited to participate in the wedding, but that they should be given a choice. If any do not want to participate, they need to be given an out. However, failing to extend an invitation to be included will probably make the children feel as though they are not wanted. It has also been my experience that most children will not only want to be present at a parent's wedding, but they will want to be involved. After all, the children are going to be part of this new family, and the wedding affects them almost as much as it does the couple.

Children of any age (except infants, perhaps), may participate. Even adult children should be invited to participate in the wedding even though it may not always be possible for older children to be present. In our mobile society, families are frequently scattered throughout the world. Nevertheless, they should be invited and not simply informed that Mom or Dad has married again.

Most of the time, I like all of the children to stand with the couple during the entire ceremony. Sometimes they can serve as attendants, but even in settings where attendants are not used, the children can still stand with the couple as part of the immediate family. During the wedding ceremony, I usually say some brief, informal words to the couple about the meaning of marriage. When there are children involved, I also include words to the children.

Following is an example of what I might say in the ceremony:

[Names], as you stand here today in the presence of God and before this gathering of family and friends, I call upon you both to truly commit your lives, each to the other. The vows you make here today express something that is holy, tender, and beautiful, for they are an expression of your love. Also, they are a commitment in which you willingly bind yourselves together for the benefit of both. This marriage is only going to be what you make it. Take it for granted and it will wither, as surely as a tender seedling that is not watered. Nourish it with love, caring, and open communication, and it will blossom beyond even your expectations. I urge you, therefore, to enter this marriage totally committed to the home that you are establishing, and may God richly bless you in it.

When there are no children involved, I leave it at that. However, when there are children, I go on to talk to the couple about the children and the need to include them in their commitment. Then I talk to the children about their involvement.

Both of you [or whatever is appropriate] enter this marriage with children: [list the children's names]. These children will have a profound effect upon your marriage. It is only with much patience, considerable effort, and a lot of love that this family is going to become what you desire. The commitment you make here is not only a commitment to each other; it is a commitment to each of the children as well.

To the children, let me say that this marriage will have an effect upon each of you as well. You can either view it as gaining another important adult person in your life with whom to share many things, or you can see it as an unwelcome intrusion. However, you are part of this family, and families function best when everyone works together. I urge you, therefore, to commit yourselves to this new family, as [the couple's names] commit themselves to each other and to you, and may the Lord God bless you all.

I never ask the children to respond. Generally, they were not involved in the decision to marry, and therefore, they should not be asked to make a commitment to something they did not choose. Nevertheless, they are involved and need to be invited to participate in a positive manner. Including the children in this way helps to get the family started as a unit, rather than with the couple and children separated.

Sherry and Dan each had three children from previous marriages, ranging in age from sixteen to five. When the children were asked if they wanted to be in the wedding, all of them said yes. Since there were three boys and three girls, arranging them next to the couple was easy. The girls would stand with Sherry, and the boys would stand with Dan. The oldest girl, Dan's daughter, would be the maid of honor and hold Dan's ring, and the oldest boy, Sherry's son, would be the best man and hold Sherry's ring. Since no favoritism was shown, the children accepted this very well.

The wedding was held at a new house that Sherry and Dan had purchased together. Family and friends (numbering close to one hundred) filled the house, and snack foods and beverages were served as the guests arrived. Music filled the house on the built-in stereo system, and the atmosphere was like a big party. Almost half an hour after the announced time of the ceremony, the guests were informed that the wedding was about to begin in the living room. Most people managed to crowd into a spot where they could see, and Dan, Sherry, the children, and the minister arranged themselves in front of the fireplace. The children were very attentive, especially when the minister spoke directly to them. Having a special place in the ceremony not only pleased them, but also made them feel like a real part of this new family. After the ceremony, the party simply continued, with Dan and Sherry cutting the wedding cake and then mingling among the guests.

Weddings can be both fun and serious. There are many ways to accomplish this, and stepfamily couples seem to be very adept at creating such events. Weddings can be inexpensive or elaborate, depending upon the preferences and resources of the couple. The wedding can either help the children become a part of the family, or it can make them feel left out. Couples should look at the wedding as an important first step of their life together.

Things to Discuss

1. Describe for your partner other weddings you have attended. What did you like and not like about each?

2. What questions or comments have the children made concerning the wedding? Have they said anything about their involvement?

3. What thoughts have you had concerning the wedding? Where would you like it to be held? Who would you like to invite? How much would you like to spend on the wedding?